16.99

BRANDO

BRANDO

ROBERT TANITCH

STUDIO
VISTA

For John Hug and Dee Hart

Studio Vista an imprint of Cassell,
Villiers House, 41/47 Strand,
London WC2N 5JE

British Library Cataloguing in Publication Data

A catalogue record for this book is available from the British Library

ISBN 0-289-80100-1
First published 1994
Copyright © Robert Tanitch 1994

The right of Robert Tanitch to be identified as author of this work has been asserted by him in accordance with the Copyright, Designs and Patents Act 1988.

Distributed in the United States by
Sterling Publishing Co. Inc.
387 Park Avenue South, New York, NY 10016-8810

Typeset by Litho Link Ltd, Welshpool, Powys, Wales

Printed and bound in Great Britain by Bath Press Limited

Frontispiece: Marlon Brando in *On the Waterfront*

Also by Robert Tanitch

A Pictorial Companion to Shakespeare's Plays

Ralph Richardson, A Tribute

Olivier

Leonard Rossiter

Ashcroft

Gielgud

Dirk Bogarde

Guinness

Sean Connery

John Mills

Contents

Introduction

Marlon Brando is acknowledged to be one of the great movie actors of the twentieth century, a legend in his lifetime. This book is a pictorial record of his career in film, theatre and television from the 1940s to the present day.

Marlon Brando has appeared in works by John Van Druten, Maxwell Anderson, Bernard Shaw, Jean Anouilh, Ben Hecht, Jean Cocteau, Tennessee Williams, John Steinbeck, William Shakespeare and adaptations of Henry James and Joseph Conrad.

He has worked with such directors as Elia Kazan, Fred Zinnemann, Joseph L. Mankiewicz, Daniel Mann, Sidney Lumet, Arthur Penn, Charles Chaplin, John Huston, Gillo Pontecorvo, Bernardo Bertolucci and Francis Ford Coppola.

He has played a wide variety of roles and been cast as poet, murderer, paraplegic, dock labourer, hooligan, emperor, bandit, mutineer, ambassador, con-man, saboteur, sheriff, gringo, Guru, kidnapper, godfather, professional killer, tycoon, civil rights lawyer, restaurateur and inquisitor.

In his films he has had an affair with a stowaway aboard a luxury liner, played dice in a New York sewer, married a dancer in Japan, fallen in love with the vicar's wife and fallen in love with a soldier, raped his sister-in-law in New Orleans and bared his buttocks in Paris.

In his time he has acted as interpreter for the American forces in the Far East and set up a private army in the Cambodian jungle, with horrific results. He has inadvertently started a civil war in South-East Asia and sparked off revolutions in Rome, Mexico and the West Indies.

He has also been strung up, beaten up, whipped, burnt to death, had his throat slit and been shot with bow and arrow . . .

Marlon Brando, the son of Marlon and Dorothy Brando, was born on 3 April 1924 in Omaha, Nebraska. His father was a sales executive and his mother, who had been a semi-professional actress, was the director of Omaha Community Theatre. He was educated in Illinois at the Lincoln School, Evanston, and at Libertyville Township School before attending Shattuck Military Academy in Fairbult, Minnesota, where he did some acting.

He went to New York in 1943 and joined Erwin Piscator's Drama Workshop at the New School for Social Research, studying under Stella Adler and acting in Gerhardt Hauptmann's dream play, *Hannele's Way to Heaven* (1944), playing the teacher and A Great Dark Angel. The *Morning Telegraph* praised his authority, smoothness, command of the stage and his careful diction. He was also seen in Molière's *Doctor Sganarelle*, Shakespeare's *Twelfth Night* (playing Viola's twin brother, Sebastian) and Stanley Kaufmann's children's play, *Bobino*, in which he was the giraffe.

Brando landed his first professional job in the theatre in 1944 when he was cast as the young son of a Norwegian–American family in John Van Druten's sentimental period piece, *I Remember Mama*, which had a two-year run on Broadway. He was twenty years old.

In 1945 he was seen in three productions: Maxwell Anderson's *Truckline Café*, playing an ex-GI who murders his unfaithful wife, Bernard Shaw's *Candida*, playing the young poet Eugene Marchbanks, opposite Katharine Cornell, and very briefly in Jean Anouilh's *Antigone*, playing the Messenger, a performance caught and admired by Laurence Olivier.

In 1946 he appreared in Ben Hecht's Jewish propaganda pageant, *A Flag is Born*, starring Paul Muni, scoring a personal success with his bitter and impassioned performance. The following year he was seen out of town in Jean Cocteau's *The Eagle Has Two Heads*, opposite Tallulah Bankhead. His role was that of a young rebel who, instead of assassinating the queen of a mythical country, fell in love with her. The queen finally goaded him into shooting her and killing himself. Bankhead had him replaced before the production came to New York.

The first night of *A Streetcar Named Desire* at the Barrymore Theatre on 3 December 1947 was a landmark in American theatre, establishing Tennessee Williams as the leading playwright of the day and making the reputations of Brando and the director, Elia Kazan. Brando remains the definitive Stanley Kowalski. The play ran for 855 performances, winning every major award, including the Pulitzer Prize, the Donaldson and the New York Drama Critics' awards.

This was to be his last appearance on the stage, except for an engagement in summer stock in 1953 when he played Sergius Saranoff in Bernard Shaw's *Arms and the Man* on a tour which included the Falmouth Playhouse in Coonamessett in Massachusetts and the Ivoryton Playhouse in Ivoryton, Connecticut. Years later, in a television interview, he would say how awful and unpleasant it had been to be on the stage: 'It wasn't that I disliked it. I hated it. I almost went out of my mind.'

Brando has, on many occasions, dismissed acting as a waste of time and a waste of a life. 'I don't find it stimulating, interesting,' he said in a television interview. 'It isn't a consuming passion.' Deeply concerned with humanitarian causes, the things which do involve him are civil rights, Third World poverty and the plight of the American Indian. 'There is no such thing

Marlon Brando in
*A Streetcar Named
Desire*

as a great movie,' he has said. 'You know what's great? A Rembrandt painting. A Mozart chamber music. These are great.'

Marlon Brando made his film debut in 1950 in a wheelchair, playing a paraplegic in the documentary–drama, *The Men*, directed by Fred Zinnemann. In order to prepare himself for the role he moved into the Birmingham Veterans Administration Hospital and lived the life of an inmate, sharing their physiotherapy.

The following year he became an instant box-office star when he recreated Stanley Kowalski in Elia Kazan's film version of *A Streetcar Named Desire* (1951), playing opposite Vivien Leigh (who had played Blanche DuBois in London), and then went on to win the best actor award at the Cannes Film Festival for his performance as Emiliano Zapata, the Mexican revolutionary, in John Steinbeck's *Viva Zapata!* (1952), which was also directed by Kazan.

There was amazement in some quarters when he was cast as Mark Antony in Joseph L. Mankiewicz's production of Shakespeare's *Julius Caesar* (1953). Actors had a field day imitating Stanley Kowalski mumbling the blank verse. In the event, his interpretation was notable, not only for its emotional urgency but also for its crystal clarity. It is a great pity that he never went on to play the older Antony, the Antony on the skids, in *Antony and Cleopatra*.

Brando, at 30, was a bit old to be playing a prototype mixed-up kid in Laslo Benedek's *The Wild One* (1954), which gained a notoriety in England when it was banned, forcing leathered rebels to jump on their motorcycles and make long journeys to screenings in the handful of cinemas up and down the country which had lifted the ban. His performance, highly mannered in its hesitancy and inarticulateness, was the quintessence of the Method school of acting; so much so that it now seems like a parody of the Method. Brando would later condemn *The Wild One* for showing the violence without trying to explain it.

His next role was one of his most famous: Terry Malone, the bum-turned-informer, in *On the Waterfront* (1954), one of the key American movies of the 1950s. Elia Kazan's intelligent and gripping production was a critical and box-office triumph, winning Oscars for best picture, best actor, best actress, best screenplay, best photography, best editing and best art direction. Kazan, carried away by the success, was quoted as saying that if there were a better performance by an actor in the history of film in America, he didn't know what it was.

The gritty realism of the waterfront was exchanged for cardboard romance in Henry Koster's *Desirée* (1954), a costume drama about Napoleon Bonaparte's love-life. The critics' headlines were fairly predictable. 'Brando Meets His Waterloo,' said the *News Chronicle*. 'No Bouquet for Napoleon,' said the *Daily Sketch*.

There was almost as much surprise in the film industry when it was announced that Brando was going to sing as there had been in the 1930s when it was announced that Greta Garbo was going to talk. There were those who thought it was a masterstroke on the part of Sam Goldwyn to cast Brando as Sky Masterson in Frank Loesser's *Guys and Dolls* (1955); others thought it merely a casting aberration. The role had orginally been intended for Gene Kelly. Eminently plausible though Brando was as a sharp, cynical, sophisticated big-time gambler, he was not so plausible as a romantic lead in a Broadway musical. There was the problem, too, about his singing.

The Teahouse of the August Moon (1956), John Patrick's Pulitzer Prize-winning satire on America spreading democracy in the Far East, should have been a musical. Brando, plump, cheerful and surprisingly boyish, played an Okinawan interpreter taking Uncle Sam for a ride. The following year he worked with Joshua Logan on *Sayonara*, an inter-racial love story, which cried out for an unhappy ending but Brando did not want it.

In 1958 he was seen in an adaptation of Irwin Shaw's *The Young Lions*, directed by Edward Dmytryk. Meticulously Germanic in looks and accent, Brando was the blondest of blond heroes, a golden god of war. He acted what should have been a brutal Nazi in an heroic and totally sympathetic manner, arguing that the brutality had been removed because nations could not go on hating the Germans long after the war had ended.

In 1960 he appeared with Anna Magnani in *The Fugitive Kind*, Sydney Lumet's adaptation of Tennessee Williams' stage play *Orpheus Descending*, cast as Val Xavier, a modern Orphic hero, a role he had turned down in the theatre. Williams never liked the film version. 'The movie,' he said, 'was so dark and so murky at times that it looked like everyone was drowning in chocolate syrup.'

When director Stanley Kubrick quit *One-Eyed Jacks* (1961) just before filming began, Brando decided to direct the western himself. The movie took six months to make. It was generally agreed that Brando, the director, had failed to discipline Brando, the actor.

Mutiny on the Bounty (1962) had a rough and expensive passage, beginning with one director (Carol Reed) and ending with another (Lewis Milestone). The movie went through innumerable scriptwriters, none of them able to get the ending right. Brando turned Fletcher Christian into a dandy with a frightfully British drawing-room comedy accent and was blamed

unfairly for practically everything that went wrong during the film's interminable shooting period.

Brando's next appearance was as an American ambassador in a contemporary political drama, *The Ugly American* (1963), which attacked US ignorance and arrogance in her relations with the Far East. The film, directed by George Englund, was way ahead of its time and unexpectedly prophetic about the Vietnam War.

He enjoyed himself in Ralph Levy's *Bedtime Story* (1964), acting opposite David Niven in a comedy which was more fun than it was given credit for being. For those who wondered what he was doing in the didactic thriller, *The Saboteur: Code Name 'Morituri'* (1965), he explained that he had three households to support and was paying alimony to two women. The film was directed by Bernhard Wicki, who had enjoyed a big success in Europe with *Die Brücke*.

Evidently much of his performance as the liberal Texan sheriff in Arthur Penn's *The Chase* (1966) ended up on the cutting-room floor. His authority and technique were, as usual, much praised but the picture is chiefly remembered, if remembered at all, for the terrible beating he received at the hands of three middle-aged thugs.

His next role was in a Western, *The Appaloosa*, also known as *Southwest to Sonora* (1966), which was directed by Sidney J. Furie, who had scored a popular hit with his 'swinging sixties' spy thriller *The Ipcress File*, starring Michael Caine. The film, under-rated by the critics and ignored by the public, had real visual flair.

The casting of Brando and Sophia Loren in Charlie Chaplin's *A Countess from Hong Kong* (1967) raised hopes, which were never realized on the screen. There were embarrassing publicity photographs in the press of the 81-year-old Chaplin, on the set, showing the stars how to act. 'We are,' Brando was reported as saying, 'sort of glorified marionettes. If he could he would play every part himself.'

John Huston's adaptation of Carson McCullers' *Reflections in a Golden Eye* (1967) left out the dreamlike poetry, but responded well to the black comedy. Brando was cast as a homosexual, a risky role for a major star to be playing in the 1960s. (The role had been earmarked for Montgomery Clift and he would have played it had he not died.) Brando, in a performance which was both painful and amusing to watch, gauged the mixture of anguish and absurdity perfectly. Many people thought it was his best picture for a very long time.

The cinema-going public had very little opportunity to see Hubert Cornfield's *The Night of the Following Day* (1969), in which he played the leader of an ill-assorted gang of kidnappers.

Marlon Brando in
The Chase

The film was shelved for a year and then released only in second-run cinemas and without publicity. The movie might have had a better critical response had it been in French and starring Yves Montand. Its rehabilitation is overdue, which is more than can be said for the picaresque *Candy* (1968), a tiresome sex odyssey by a teenage nymphomaniac, dismissed by the *News of the World* as 'a second-rate outrageous tease' and by the *People* as 'a pornographic eyeful'.

Queimada! (*Burn!*, 1970), one of the major movies of the 1970s though not recognized as such at the time, was a flawed yet powerful indictment of colonization, capitalism and political expediency by Gillo Pontecorvo, the Marxist director of the much admired *The Battle of Algiers*. Its rehabilitation is also long overdue.

Michael Winner then cast him as Peter Quint in *The Nightcomers* (1971), which revealed what had led up to the events described by Henry James in his famous ghost story, *The Turn of the Screw*.

A major turning point in Brando's career came with the release of the film version of Mario Puzo's bestselling novel, *The Godfather* (1972), directed by Francis Ford Coppola, a key picture of the 1970s, hailed by *Newsweek* as 'the *Gone with the Wind* of gangster movies' and the biggest Mafia soap opera ever made. 'Never since Goebbels,' wrote Fergus Cashin in the *Sun*, 'has the propaganda of violence been so beautifully put together.' In the relatively small part of the godfather his performance dominated the picture. It was one of the great comebacks in American film history. His portrait of Don Corleone, a tyrant dreaming of respectability while dwindling into senility, was both lethal and tender, dangerous yet benevolent. It was an offer the American Academy of Motion Picture Act and Sciences clearly could not refuse and he won an Oscar, which was declined on his behalf by an Apache in full tribal dress at the presentation ceremony itself.

For some people his performance in *L'Ultimo Tango A Parigi* (*Last Tango in Paris*, 1972) was even better; certainly it was the most autobiographical and revealing of all his roles. Pauline Kael, critic of the *New Yorker*, compared the screening she saw at the New York Film Festival on 14 October 1972 to the first performance of Igor Stravinsky's *Le Sacré du Printemps* on 29 May 1913. 'This must be the most powerfully erotic movie ever made,' she wrote. 'Bertolucci and Brando have altered the face of an art form.' *Tango* was banned in Italy. Director Bernando Bertolucci and the two stars, Brando and Maria Schneider, were indicted on a charge of obscenity in Bologna, a charge carrying a sentence of between three months and

three years. British cinemagoers (and pornographers) who wanted to see the film initially had to make special trips to Paris where it was running in eight cinemas. Mary Whitehouse called for the resignation of the entire Board of British Film censors after they had passed the film and made only one ten-second cut. *Tango* was a huge box-office hit and Brando received his seventh Oscar nomination. In 1978 the Italians burned all their prints except for three copies, which were consigned to the National Film Library.

He was cast as the coldblooded manhunter in *The Missouri Breaks* (1976), an under-rated Western directed by Arthur Penn. Acting opposite Jack Nicholson, Brando's flamboyant performance came in for more adverse reviews than it deserved, some critics seeing only outrageous indiscipline, self-parody and disdain. He then went on to play Superman's boring old dad in the prologue to Richard Donner's *Superman* (1978), to which he brought nothing except his bankable name.

Apocalypse Now (1979) was based on Joseph Conrad's *The Heart of Darkness* and is one of the great cinema statements on war. Francis Ford Coppola transposed Conrad's mythical and metaphysical novella from the Congo of the 1890s to Vietnam, intending to shed light on what that war had done to all those involved in it. Brando was cast as Kurtz, the civilized man turned monster, a role he initially had turned down. Conrad had described Kurtz as a monumental character struggling with the extremities of his soul, a description Brando (looking like 'an enormous animated image of death carved out of old ivory') more than matched. There were those, however, who found the mystical final sequence protracted, pretentious and an anti-climax.

Brando shortly afterwards made a rare television appearance, his first since the late 1940s, playing George Lincoln Rockwell, the American Nazi Party leader, in Alex Hayley's *Roots: The Next Generations* (1979), the second series of the immensely popular television production. He won an Emmy (television's equivalent of an Oscar) for outstanding supporting actor.

He had a small part in *The Formula* (1980), Steve Shagan's international conspiracy thriller, cast as the villain opposite George C. Scott's hero; but the hoped for fireworks between the two actors never materialized.

Nine years later he played another small but more crucial part, the civil rights lawyer in the South African anti-apartheid movie, *A Dry White Season* (1989), directed by the black woman director, Euzhan Palcy, who had achieved international success with her first feature film, *La Rue Cases Nègres* (*Sugar Cane Alley*). Brando won favourable reviews but the film itself was generally dismissed as a banal and lifeless political thriller. He also scored a palpable hit in Andrew Bergman's likeable Mafia spoof, *The Freshman* (1990), in which he gave a gentle and amusing parody of his Don Corleone performance in *The Godfather*.

His last film to date was the inept and risible *Christopher Columbus – The Discovery* (1992), directed by John Glen, in which he played Torquemada, a not very grand Grand Inquisitor, who remained on the periphery of the action.

Marlon Brando is one of the major talents of the cinema, the finest actor of his generation, his acting skills admired by critics, cinemagoers and, above all, his peers. His revolutionary screen technique changed the whole conception of film acting. The following pages are both a pictorial record and a tribute to him: a reminder of his authority, physical presence, magnetism, dynamism, versatility and the pleasure his performances have given.

The 1940s

I REMEMBER MAMA

By John Van Druten   Directed by John Van Druten
Music Box Theatre   1944

I Remember Mama was based on Kathryn Forbes' *Mama's Bank Account* and described incidents in the lives of a Norwegian–American family in San Francisco at the turn of the century. The play was praised for its warmth, honesty and universal humour. Marlon Brando was cast as the 25-year-old son of the house who wanted to be a doctor.

The Nels of Marlon Brando is, if he doesn't mind my saying so, charming.

Robert Garland, *New York Journal-American*

Mady Christians,
Marlon Brando,
Joan Tetzel,
Nancy Marquand,
Carolyn Hummel and
Richard Bishop in
I Remember Mama

TRUCKLINE CAFÉ

By Maxwell Anderson   Directed by Harold Clurman
Belasco Theatre   1946

I haven't seen such acting since John
Barrymore. It was terrific. It was inside of him
– a psychic explosion.

Harold Clurman

The setting was a West Coast diner. Marlon
Brando played a World War II veteran who
murders his unfaithful wife (off-stage) and
then waits (on-stage) for the cops to arrive.
  The critics did not like the play. Maxwell
Anderson took a full-page advertisement to
answer them. 'The public is far better
qualified to judge plays than the men who
write reviews for our dailies,' he wrote. 'It is
an insult to our theatre that there should be so
many incompetents and irresponsibles among
them.' The play closed after thirteen
performances.

**Marlon Brando and Ann Shepherd bear the brunt
of the melodrama with considerable skill.**

Howard Barnes, *Herald Tribune*

**As the young murderer Marlon Brando is quite
effective in a difficult emotional scene.**

Louis Kronenberger, *PM*

**Except for a brief bit by Marlon Brando as the
former solider who blew his top, the acting was
indifferently bad.**

Burton Rascoe, *New York World-Telegram*

Virginia Gilmore,
Robert Simon and
Marlon Brando in
Truckline Café

CANDIDA

By Bernard Shaw   Directed by Guthrie McClintic
Cort Theatre   1946

Marlon Brando and
Katharine Cornell
in *Candida*

Eugene Marchbanks (Marlon Brando), the
18-year-old aesthete, a snivelling, cowardly
whelp, falls in love with Mrs Morell
(Katharine Cornell), the wife of a socialist
minister (Cedric Hardwicke), moralist and
windbag, who is in love with preaching.
Marchbanks insists she choose between
them. She chooses the weaker man. Her
husband is surprised to find she means him.

Katharine Cornell declared that Brando,
when he was at his best, was the finest
Marchbanks she had acted opposite.

**Young Mr Brando stepped right out of the stage
directions.**

Robert Garland, *New York Journal-American*

**Mr Brando achieved a believable, lovesick
introvert by playing very quietly. His intensity was
within him, where it should be.**

John Chapman, *New York Daily News*

A FLAG IS BORN

By Ben Hecht with music by Kurt Weill
Directed by Luther Adler   Alvin Theatre   1946

Produced by the American League for a Free
Palestine, *A Flag is Born* was a propaganda
pageant. Kurt Weill's score was liked and so
was Paul Muni's performance in the leading
role. Ben Hecht's script on the other hand was
not liked, most critics finding the play a
wearisome lecture.

Marlon Brando played a young Jew who
joined the underground fighters, convinced
that a Jewish homeland could be won only by
militant Judaism.

**Paul Muni, Celia Adler and Marlon Brando
obviously feel deeply the gravity of their message
and their performances as the tortured trio in the
graveyard are dignified and impressive.**

Wolcott Gibbs, *New Yorker*

**Marlon Brando, the young actor who was so
generally acclaimed last season, is a bitter and
impassioned David.**

Ward Morehouse, *New York Sun*

Marlon Brando in
A Flag is Born

A STREETCAR NAMED DESIRE

By Tennessee Williams   Directed by Elia Kazan
Barrymore Theatre   1947

Every man is a king and I'm king around here, and don't you forget it.

Stanley Kowalski

A Streetcar Named Desire was a landmark in American theatre, establishing author, director, actor and the Method. The play won every major honour, including the Pulitzer Prize, the Donaldson and the New York Drama Critics' awards.

Miss Tandy is brilliantly supported by Marlon Brando as Stan, who brings a fierce passionate violence to the scene.

Rosamund Gildes, *Theatre Arts*

Marlon Brando, as Kowalski, is, as hinted previously, almost pure ape (his sister-in-law's description of him as 'common' entertained me quite a lot, there in the dark) and though he undoubtedly emphasizes the horrors of the Vieux Carré as opposed to Belle Rêve, it is a brutally effective characterization.

Wolcott Gibbs, *New Yorker*

Brando is our theatre's most memorable young actor at his most memorable.

Robert Garland, *New York Journal-American*

No one is likely to under-rate Marlon Brando's brilliant performance as the brother-in-law, the more astonishing for being like nothing else he has ever played.

Louis Kronenberger, *PM*

Mr Brando is magnificent as the forthright husband, in his simple rages, his simple affections and his blunt humour.

John Chapman, *Daily News*

Previous pages:
Peg Hillias, Kim Hunter, Rudy Bond, Richard Garrick, Jessica Tandy, Karl Malden, Nick Dennis, Marlon Brando and Ann Dere in
A Streetcar Named Desire

Marlon Brando and Jessica Tandy in
A Streetcar Named Desire

The 1950s

Marlon Brando in
The Wild One

THE MEN

Directed by Fred Zinnemann   1950
Alternative title: *Battle Stripe*

He was not only a great actor, but a shattering force of nature. He had a volcanic quality that seemed essential for 'our' hero.

Fred Zinnemann, *An Autobiography*

The Men was set in a US hospital for war veterans, paralysed from the waist down and, in most cases, impotent and sentenced to a life in a wheelchair. The opening lecturette spelled out to mothers, wives, fiancées and girlfriends what it meant to be a paraplegic.

The film, a sincere and sentimental documentary with a happy ending, concentrated on one man, Ken Wilozek (Marlon Brando), a former infantry lieutenant, and his devoted fiancée, Ellen (Teresa Wright). The movie described his long battle to adjust himself physically and psychologically.

Carl Foreman's script was clichéd and heavy-handed. Teresa Wright had to say things like 'I'm not marrying a wheelchair, I am marrying a man,' whilst wisecracking Jack Webb (playing a patient who didn't want to be rehabilitated and take his proper place in society) had to say things like 'To be or not to be that is the question'. Everybody in the ward was a comedian. Everybody was a cynic.

There was an over-dramatized incident in a restaurant with the patrons staring rudely at the couple in the most unlikely manner. The scene between Ellen and her parents was equally contrived. 'Is it so wrong for us to want a grandchild?' they pleaded. There was also an encounter with a drunk, a World War I veteran. 'I want to apologize,' said Wilozek, predictably apologizing with a punch on the jaw.

At the wedding ceremony the groom was so determined to stand up that he nearly fell over during the responses. The wedding night was an absurdly stagey disaster, the quarrel artificially engineered. 'I don't like the way you are looking at me,' said Wilozek, who was having to cope with a squeaking wheelchair, shaking legs, spilt champagne and, if that were not enough, also a photographic album full of pictures of himself when he was young, fit and healthy, playing football. 'Are you thinking you made a mistake?' asked Ellen. 'All right, I am,' he replied, returning to the hospital to rejoin the other paraplegics in the TV room, which he then proceeded to smash up.

Insulated behind a wall of sullen embitterment, Brando raged inwardly and outwardly at his impotence, forcing the audience to share his pain. The reunion with his fiancée was deeply moving: 'Will you get out. [In tears] Who asked you to pity me? There is no hope. The wires are cut.'

The first time Wilozek made a conscious effort to lift himself off his back, Dimitri Tiomkin's score behaved as if it were leading into the show-stopping number of a Broadway hit musical. Obtrusive and inappropriate, the music was insulting to the actor. Brando didn't need it. His acting in its subtle and realistic changes from despair to hope and back again was powerful enough and, contrary to what many critics said at the time, totally audible.

The doctor's frustration that he could not cure his patients and his exasperation and anger at the men who expected his help yet

Marlon Brando and
Teresa Wright in
The Men

30

His face, the whole rhythm of his body and especially the strange timbre of his voice, often broken and plaintive and boyish, are articulate every way. Out of stiff and frozen silences he can lash into a passionate rage with the fearful and flailing frenzy of a taut cable suddenly cut.

Bosley Crowther, *The New York Times*

He turns out to be a giant with the face of a poet and the build of a heavyweight boxer and I have no hesitation in naming him the most interesting new actor Hollywood has shown us this year. I don't think he's quite at home with the camera yet. But he has a fiery gleam in his eye, a way of rolling his lines round his tongue and then spitting them out as if he meant every word, which promise well.

Star

Teresa Wright and
Marlon Brando in
The Men

refused to help themselves was expressed in the most theatrical manner by Everett Sloane, who nevertheless got an excellent press. *The Times* and *Daily Express* critics thought he was the best thing in the film.

Forty-five men of the Birmingham Veterans Administration Hospital played themselves, including the charismatic Arthur Juardo, who was cast as the most likeable patient in the ward, the one with the splendid torso, who died.

The film depends a good deal, of course, on Marlon Brando, whose combination of style, depth and range comes like a blood transfusion into cinema acting.

Richard Winnington, *Sight and Sound*

I don't suppose anyone could improve on Mr Brando's performance in *The Men*. Even as a handicapped veteran, he seems so authentically overpowering physically that he makes most standard Hollywood heroes look like flyweights.

John McCarten, *New Yorker*

Broadway's Marlon Brando, in his first movie, does a magnificent job. His halting, mumbled delivery, glowering silences and expert simulation of paraplegia do not suggest acting at all; they look chillingly like the real thing.

Time Magazine

Teresa Wright, Marlon
Brando and Everett
Sloane in *The Men*

He is handsome in a virile way and looks as though he may amount to something quite big when he gets more used to the new technique.

Jympson Harman, *Evening News*

32

A STREETCAR NAMED DESIRE

Directed by Elia Kazan   1951

A Streetcar Named Desire is an extremely and peculiarly moral play, in the deepest and truest sense of the term. The rape of Blanche by Stanley is a pivotal integral truth in the play without which the play loses its meaning, which is the ravishment of the tender, the sensitive, the delicate by the savage and brutish forces of modern society. It is a poetic plea for comprehension.

Tennessee Williams
in a letter to the Censor, Joseph Breen

A Streetcar Named Desire was a record of a stage performance: a studio-bound translation of Tennessee Williams's harsh and powerful poetic drama, faithful in spirit, though not (as a result of the Hayes Code and Legion of Decency) always faithful to the letter.

Blanche DuBois (Vivien Leigh), a faded Southern belle, a much-battered butterfly, who always had had to rely on the kindness of strangers, saw herself as a heroine in a play by Alexander Dumas. 'I don't want realism,' she said, 'I want magic.'

Blanche came to New Orleans to stay with her sister, Stella (Kim Hunter) and Stella's husband, Stanley Kowalski (Brando). She was horrified by the squalor of the Vieux Carré.

Revolted by Stanley, yet attracted to him, she outstayed her welcome by five months, constantly attempting to break up his marriage, arguing that he was common and like an animal and pleading with her sister 'not to hang back with the brutes'. Stanley took his revenge, dragging up her past and stripping her gentle, middle-aged suitor, Mitch (Karl Malden) of his illusions.

Marlon Brando and
Vivien Leigh in
*A Streetcar Named
Desire*

35

Vivien Leigh's Blanche, vulnerable and frightened, was a pathetic figure. The actress captured most movingly the self-dramatization and those wretched and often embarrassing displays of vanity and gentility. Harry Stradling's photography, in all its unflattering lighting, in its dark and steamy monochrome, paid the performance the highest compliment, registering the played-out decadence beneath the frailty.

Alex North gave the melodramatic hysterics an unashamedly operatic-jazzy score and Blanche's long arias were brilliantly orchestrated and punctuated by an assortment of sound effects: rain, thunder, trains, revolver shots, laughter, screams and bells.

Marlon Brando was and still is the definitive Stanley Kowalski: a caged animal in a dirty, sweaty T-shirt, confident in his sex appeal, boozing, gambling, bullying, breaking up the furniture and finally raping Blanche while his wife was in hospital giving birth to their baby.

Everybody remembers the brutality, the cruelty, the sheer loutishness: the way he gave Blanche a one-way ticket as a birthday present, the sudden eruption of frightening violence when he hurled the radio out of the window and cleared his place at table by sweeping the crockery onto the floor. ('My place is cleared. You want me to clear yours?') What is, perhaps, forgotten is the ironic humour and sensitivity of the performance.

His first encounter with Blanche was witty. ('I guess I must strike you as being the unrefined type.') He immediately sussed her

Kim Hunter and Marlon Brando in *A Streetcar Named Desire*

out, and bemused, taunted her. Yet Brando was never entirely unsympathetic and he could be surprisingly tender in his scenes with his wife. There was a memorable moment when, his face and body dripping wet, his shirt hanging off his shoulders, he burst into tears of shame and bellowed 'STELLAHHHH!' in the courtyard, like a wounded bull.

Kim Hunter and Karl Malden, repeating their stage performances, were excellent, winning Oscars for the best supporting actress and best supporting actor. Vivien Leigh won the best actress award. Brando was nominated but lost to Humphrey Bogart in *The African Queen.*

Marlon Brando in *A Streetcar Named Desire*

37

Marlon Brando and
Vivien Leigh in
*A Streetcar Named
Desire*

Brilliantly and brutally played he recreates the character he played with such magnetic force on the Broadway stage, and if his speech is sometimes quite incoherent his performance is too meaty to require such trimmings as words.

Cecil Wilson, *Daily Mail*

As the hulking animalistic Kowalski, Marlon Brando fills his scenes with a virile power that gives *Streetcar* its highest voltage.

Time Magazine

If any man can harness atomic energy Mr Brando is the chap for the job.

Jympson Harman, *Evening News*

As Kowalski, Marlon Brando is terrifyingly good.

Manchester Guardian

Mr Brando is alternatively funny and terrifying as the muscular Pole, whose social habits might raise eyebrows even in Brownsville.

John McCarten, *New Yorker*

Marlon Brando, as Stanley Kowalski, represents probably the lowest common denominator yet to be presented seriously in motion pictures. His uncouth, physical crudity is fascinatingly repulsive. It is a shocking, but memorable characterisation.

Milton Shulman, *Evening Standard*

After seeing his graphically visualised performance, you will have had a glimpse of what relations between the sexes must have been like in the Stone Age. . . . I shall think *Streetcar* is not so much a play as a dramatised Apache dance. . . . It excites no pity. It draws no tears. But it is something to go and watch in horrid fascination.

Leonard Mosley, *Daily Express*

Previous pages:
Vivien Leigh and
Marlon Brando in
*A Streetcar Named
Desire*

40

VIVA ZAPATA!

Directed by Elia Kazan   1952

I don't want to be the conscience of the world.
I don't want to be the conscience of anybody.

Emiliano Zapata

The early 1950s were the days of Senator McCarthy's witch-hunt and many a Hollywood career had been finished by the Committee of Un-American Activities. Elia Kazan himself, vulnerable to charges of being a communist, went to great lengths to make certain that *Viva Zapata!* would not be seen as a communist tract.

Viva Zapata!, a mixture of truth and legend, presented scenes from the Mexican Revolution and was a political statement on the corruption of power. John Steinbeck's screenplay, realistic and symbolic, was not always helped by his ponderous dialogue; even the light relief, provided by a courting couple exchanging proverbs, proved heavy going. Lines like 'A strong man makes a weak people. Strong people don't need a strong man' are liable to defeat even the best actors. Much more effective were the economical scenes of action: the massacre of the peasants in the fields, the attack on the train and the storming of the garrison.

There were three memorable set-pieces. The first was the arrest and rescue of Zapata by the peasants emerging from the country-side, more and more of them converging on the police escort, marching alongside them, until the escort was totally surrounded and brought to a standstill.

The second was the assassination of Modera, the idealistic and much loved yet

Marlon Brando in
Viva Zapata!

totally ineffective President. Harold Gordon (a first-rate performance) played him as a bearded mouse in a black suit, a quiet, scholarly and harassed man. His murderer was the sinister future dictator, General Huerta (Frank Silvera), a frightening, massive, bullet-headed, cigar-smoking villain.

The third sequence was the carefully planned ambush and murder of Zapata, lured into a trap by the promise of guns and ammunition. The actual moment of betrayal, with a Judas-like kiss by a nervous Colonel (Frank De Cova), was admirably staged and edited, Zapata's beautiful white horse snorting as she sensed the danger.

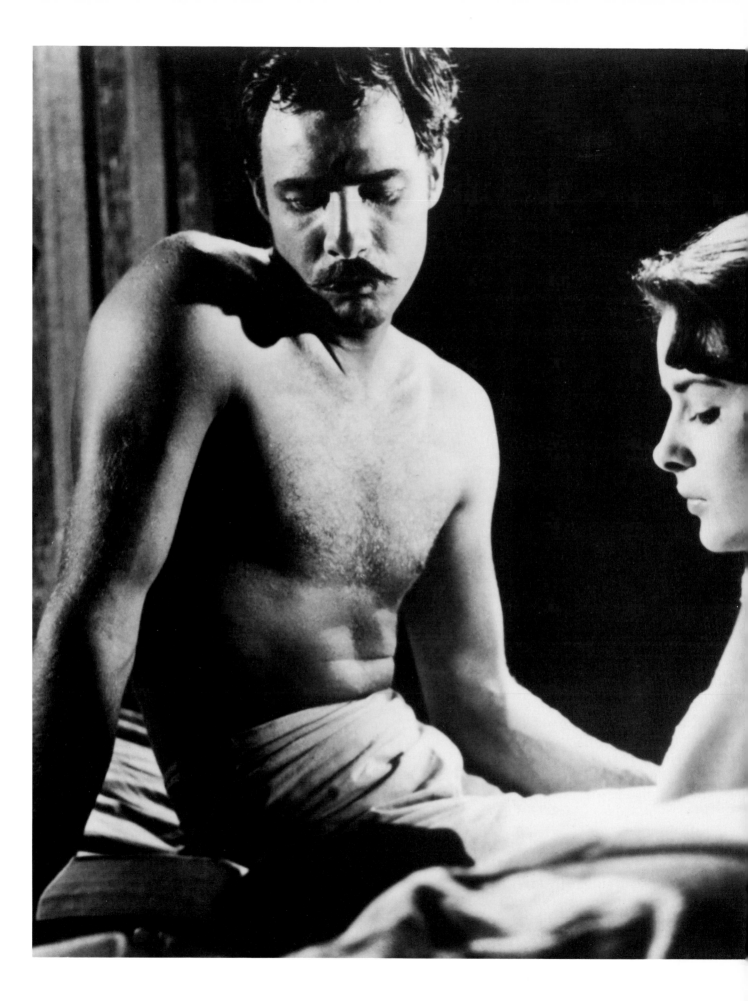

Kazan's groupings and framings were always self-consciously picturesque. The bodies and faces, dramatically lit, had a sculptural impact, recalling the work of the great Russian film director, Sergei Eisenstein. This was particularly true of the tableaux of Zapata's dead brother (Anthony Quinn) and Zapata's own bullet-riddled body lying in the square. The excellent camerawork was by Joe MacDonald.

With a two-way stretch inside his mouth, his eyelids glued together at the edges and plastic rings in his nose, Marlon Brando looked nothing like the Brando of *The Men* and the Brando of *A Streetcar Named Desire*. He might have stepped out of a mural by Diego Rivera. Some critics thought he looked as Mexican as an Aztec; others, less enthusiastic, were reminded of Charlie Chan in a sombrero.

Brando's Zapata, illiterate, brooding, taciturn, passionately dedicated to land reform, was an idealized portrait of a man, who immediately established his honesty on his first appearance when a delegation of Indians came to Mexico City in 1909 for an audience with President Diaz. Years later, Zapata's integrity was such that the moment he saw that he too was being corrupted by power, he rejected the presidency and headed back home. Brando's performance was notable not only for its smouldering power and magnificent physique but also for its sullen, stubborn and moral superiority.

The real Zapata always got his priorities right. The revolution first; women second. He was credited with over 1,100 executions and well over twenty bigamous marriages. The

Marlon Brando and
Jean Peters in
Viva Zapata!

43

Anthony Quinn,
Marlon Brando,
Lou Gilbert and
Harold Gordon in
Viva Zapata!

film limited itself to just one marriage, with bride (Jean Peters) and groom finding a most original way of spending their wedding night. 'I can't read,' he said. 'Teach me. Teach me NOW. Get a book.'

Marlon Brando's Zapata is a magnificent performance. No smaller word can intimate its stature, unless one is prepared to take it at its proper value, the simple word 'great'. Acting of Mr Brando's sort is not seen often nowadays in the cinema. It marks the triumph of intelligence over exhibitionism.

C.A. Lejeune, *Observer*

With this performance he confirms the belief that he is the most interesting young actor Hollywood has discovered in years.

Roy Nash, *Star*

Arguments as to whether or not Brando can act in the theatrical sense are irrelevant. Brando conveys power, which, in the cinema, can transcend acting – as in *Streetcar* he transcended Vivien Leigh. Here it is the power of an illiterate Indian given to few words, whose rare, swift eloquence can startle, whose rage can scorch – the power to rouse, lead and safeguard a whole countryside.

Richard Winnington, *News Chronicle*

So far his acting repertoire has been confined somewhere between the illiterate and the explosive. Zapata proves he can do it wearing a sombrero. But the ability to scowl, to shrug sullenly and to shout without parting the lips hardly adds up to a Mexican bandit. Mr Brando still has to prove he is good at something other than Mr Brando.

Milton Shulman, *Evening Standard*

JULIUS CAESAR

Directed by Joseph L. Mankiewicz   1953

How many ages hence
Shall this our lofty scene be acted over
In states unborn and accents yet unknown!

Julius Caesar, Act III, Scene 1

Julius Caesar was generally thought to be the best Shakespeare Hollywood had yet produced and surprised everybody by doing better business at the box office than *Quo Vadis?*

Producer John Houseman (who had worked with Orson Welles on the Mercury Theatre's modern-dress production back in the 1930s) described the film as a political thriller; yet despite the presence of Louis Calherne and Edmund O'Brien, whose casting as Caesar and Casca certainly suggested a gangster movie, circa 44 BC, there were few thrills.

Shot in black and white, no concessions whatsoever were made to the mass audience.

Louis Calhern,
Marlon Brando and
Greer Garson in
Julius Caesar

Mankiewicz concentrated on the text and the acting, which was seen mostly in close-up. So keen was everybody not to offend Shakespeare purists that the film actually looked like a photographed stage production, reverential and dull. Expectations that Mark Antony (given to wildness and late nights) might be seen running naked through the city, tapping barren women with his thong, were quickly dashed. There was no distraction from the words. The actors were never anywhere but in a studio, speaking their lines with commendable clarity in a total vacuum. There was no spectacle and little cinema. The Battle of Philippi was no more than a Red Indian ambush in a Californian gully, straight out of a B-movie western.

Brando's virile Antony certainly looked the most Roman of them all; and though he acted in a different style from James Mason (a much under-rated Brutus) and John Gielgud (whose Cassius, lean and hungry, had come hotfoot from Stratford), he was unmistakably the shrewd contriver and ruthless avenger the Shakespearian text demands. There was never any doubt of the danger he threatened. The depth of his love and his grief for the death of Caesar were passionately expressed.

In the famous 'Friends, Romans, country-men' oration in the Forum, he had the odd difficulty with a word like 'interr'd', but his real problem was that the speech had been chopped up and he had to play to the camera rather than the crowd; and whenever there were shots of the crowd (surprisingly sparse, stagey and ineffectual), they were so obviously slotted into his rhetoric as to rob the scene of its dramatic impact.

Brando's Mark Antony, shouting himself hoarse, was so patently disposed to mutiny, notably in his huge, rallying cry, 'WHENCE COMES SUCH ANOTHER?' (clearly modelled on Laurence Olivier's Henry V) that the omission of a line like 'Now let it work' and the murder of Cinna were inexplicable. There was, however, one moment when the screen did have the edge over the stage and that was when Antony turned his back on the crowd and the camera was able to catch the un-guarded and smug smile of a demagogue, con-temptuous of the ease of his success.

If audiences wondered why the earlier soliloquy over the dead body of Caesar was so much more thrilling in its emotional drive and energy, confidently building to a tremendous climax on 'CRY HAVOC!', perhaps the answer, in part, might well have been that he had been coached by Gielgud, England's foremost classical actor, in the first scene but not the second.

There is no question in my mind that in natural equipment, temperament and application, he is one of the very great actors of our time.

John Houseman, *Theatre Arts Monthly*

Here is not Shakespearian verse spoken as the Cassius of Sir John Gielgud speaks it; here, rather, is a sullen, dangerous and explosive force which will electrify those to whom Shakespeare represents a dreary task learnt in a forgotten classroom. This *Julius Caesar* is not Shakespeare vulgarised; it is, however, Shakespeare immediate and exciting.

The Times

James Mason and Marlon Brando in *Julius Caesar*

Marlon Brando's achievement as Mark Antony is sensational, for nobody could confidently have expected him to travel by *Streetcar* into Shakespeare's Rome. His speeches over dead Caesar in the Forum are a magnificent mixture of brimming anger and grief, and self-steadying diplomacy; and the great oration to the Roman mob is shot through with new and vital meaning.

Sydney Morning Herald

Happily, Mr Brando's diction, which has been guttural and slurred in previous films, is clear and precise in this instance. In him a major talent has emerged.

Bosley Crowther, *The New York Times*

Marlon Brando, as Mark Antony, plainly shows he needs a bit of speech training before he can graduate into an acting league where the spoken word is a trifle more significant than the flexed biceps and the fixed eye.

John McCarten, *New Yorker*

Marlon Brando in
Julius Caesar

THE WILD ONE

Directed by Laslo Benedek   1954

> The subject isn't juvenile delinquency. Its's youth without ideals, without goals, which doesn't know what to do with its enormous energy.
>
> Laslo Benedek

The Wild One, a would-be serious American study of violence and authority, was based on an incident in 1947 when 4,000 motor cyclists wrecked a small Californian town. The opening sequence showed the Black Rebels Motor Cycle Club advancing down an empty road, hooligans on wheels, in search of excitement. The gang looked like so many extras, some of them seemingly old enough to have appeared in the *Dead End Kids* movies of the 1930s.

The film was banned in Britain. The refusal to give it a certificate stemmed from the fear that its depiction of hooligans and violence might incite adolescents to imitate them. All the ban did was to give *The Wild One* an importance it never had in the first place.

The ban was not lifted until 1968 and by then the movie, which belonged to the era of *The Blackboard Jungle* and *Rebel Without a Cause*, looked like a parody of its former self, more reminiscent of the 1930s and 1940s than the 1950s. Nobody could quite see what all the fuss had been about. It almost had a period charm. 'The Mild One' said the wits and compared it unfavourably to Roger Corman's newer *The Wild Angels*.

Brando was cast as Johnny, the gang's taciturn leader. 'What are you rebelling

Mary Murphy and Marlon Brando in *The Wild One*

50

Marlon Brando and
Mary Murphy in
The Wild One

Previous pages:
Hugh Sanders, Robert
Keith, Jay C. Flippen
and Marlon Brando in
The Wild One

warning, immediately identified with
Johnny's message ('Nobody tells me what to
do. . . . Nobody is too good for me. . . . I don't
like cops') and went out and got the black
leather gear and bikes.

John Paxton's screenplay blamed the town
for the violence as much as it blamed the
youths. The terrified citizens turned fascist
and Johnny was beaten up and very nearly
lynched. Finally, ordered out of the state by
the sheriff (Jay C. Flippen), he handed over a
stolen statuette (his phallus) to the waitress,
who had loved and redeemed him.

An earlier love scene with the same
waitress (Mary Murphy), in a horribly stagey
studio glade, was unintentionally comic. The
shots of her fondling his cycle, reeling in
ecstasy and the enormous close-ups of her
face only increased the laughter.

**The Wild One has never done well at the box
office: it is a minority cult. How far Brando's
magnetism has brought about this cult is anybody's
guess. Certainly his performance as Johnny is the
film's only visible artistry. With its sly yet mannered
delivery, and its pantherine grace, it conveys a
sense of great force held in check.**

Eric Rhode, *Listener*

**Marlon Brando's celebrated performance turns out
to be a run-of-the-mill study in sullen impudence –
steel under black leather – but the final angelic
smile as he repentantly roars away into the dusk
sells the character short. Benedek's film is
ultimately moral, but something of a pain into the
bargain.**

David Castell, *Londoner*

against?' asked one local girl. 'What you
got?' he replied. Brando projected the macho
image in full: dark glasses, leather jacket, cap
at an effeminate angle, the lazy tilt of the
head, the swaggering insolence, the cocky
walk, the smouldering sensuality. The latter
was crudely emphasized by his smashing a
bottle down on the counter and letting the
booze foam all over the rim.

There were lots of close-ups of the actor,
pin-up fashion, staring impassively at the
camera, brooding poetically, sending out all
sorts of ambiguous messages, not least about
his relationship with a rival gang leader,
Chino (Lee Marvin). 'Hi ja, sweetheart.
Johnny, I love you,' said Chino, playing
Mercutio to Brando's Romeo.

Brando's inarticulation was so articulate
that disaffected youth, far from heeding the

ON THE WATERFRONT

Directed by Elia Kazan   1954

It's a film about the necessity in certain circumstances of speaking out. It shows, in this precise circumstance, how the attitude of keeping quiet was harmful on the waterfront. It's a true story, we did not exaggerate anything. It happened like that.

Elia Kazan, quoted by Claudine Tavernier, *Cinema*

On the Waterfront had its roots in Malcolm Johnson's Pulitzer Prize-winning series of investigative articles into organized crime in New York's dockland, which had appeared in the New York *Sun* in 1949. The film was in the tradition of the 1930s gangster movie with a social message and it protested as loudly against corruption and tyranny in the unions as Clifford Odets' famous agitprop drama, *Waiting for Lefty*, had done at The Group Theatre in 1935. The screenplay was a powerful indictment of the way the union controlled all employment, extorting crippling dues and murdering anybody who stood up to them.

Marlon Brando played Terry Malone, an ex-prize fighter, pushing 30, who was the Mob's errand boy and hanger-on, too stupid to realize what was really going on until the murder of a worker awakened his conscience.

Terry fell in love with the murder victim's sister. His gauche courting of Edie in the children's park – the shrugging of the shoulder, the gum-chewing, the disarming smile, the confidence in his machismo – all this was beautifully played, sensitive and humorous. There was, too, that unforgettable moment when he picked up and put on her glove (a glove which the actress had dropped

by mistake) and put it to subtle, sexy use.

All Brando's scenes with Eva Marie Saint (excellent as Edie) worked well. When the time came for him to confess his part in the murder, Kazan used a fog-horn to drown their dialogue, the wailing scoring Edie's hysteria.

It wasn't until the murder of his own brother (last seen hanging from a meat-hook) that Terry was finally pushed into standing up to the Mob and testifying before the Crimes Commission, an act which led to his total ostracism by the work force.

Brando, tough yet likeable, deftly suggested a confused, essentially decent young man trying to work things out. The inarticulateness, with all its hestitations, coughs, repetitions and the overlapping dialogue, has often been parodied but, at the time of the film's release,

Marlon Brando and Karl Malden in *On the Waterfront*

Eva Marie Saint and Marlon Brando in *On the Waterfront*

57

Rod Steiger and
Marlon Brando in
On the Waterfront

Karl Malden,
Marlon Brando and
Eva Marie Saint in
On the Waterfront

it was new and very convincing, a classic
example of Method.

On the Waterfront ended with a brutal fight
in which Terry was given a terrible beating,
which was observed by Edie, the local priest
(Karl Malden) and the dockers (played by
actors and real dockers), all of whom did
nothing. The fight was then followed by a
heroic stagger to the sheds and still nobody
helped him as he led the men back to work.
There was even a theatrical 'curtain' when
the door closed behind them. It was the
script's major false moment, far too heroic to
ring true. The movie should have ended with
Terry Malone's death.

Lee J. Cobb played the ugly union boss in a
loud-mouthed manner which was way over
the top, yet not any the less effective for that.
It was his stereotyped henchmen who were
unacceptable, looking and acting like
caricatures out of a *Dick Tracy* cartoon.

Rod Steiger was cast as Charley Malone,
the union boss's right-hand man. He shared
the much-quoted scene in the back of a car,
when he was condemned by Terry, his
younger brother: 'Oh Charley . . . Oh Charley
. . . You don't understand. I could have had
class. I could have been a contender. I could
have been somebody, instead of a bum, which
is what I am.'

Kazan shot the film on location in winter and Boris Kaufman's photography (the dockers' breath steaming in the early morning winter cold), had a gritty newsreel quality. Leonard Bernstein's music gave the melodrama a *West Side Story* punch and lyricism.

It is one of the most moving pieces of acting I have ever seen.

Roy Nash, *Star*

Mr Brando is the only actor in the world who can make unintelligibility sound like poetry. Nor is there any other actor I have seen who, at one and the same moment, can reach for the stars and wallow in the gutter.

Beverley Baxter, *Evening Standard*

His basically decent, inarticulate dumb-ox is high art — meticulous, subtle character acting. To take an eye off him for a second is to miss something vital and telling.

Stephen Watts, *Sunday Chronicle*

Mr Brando has a number of astonishing *tours de force* to his credit but this must surely be his subtlest performance — the slow awakening, the groping for the truth is brilliantly done.

Fred Majdalany, *Time and Tide*

This is the best sort of screen acting, always working inward, not building up, but chiselling away from the rock until we see the author's creation full size, and with all that is irrelevant cast aside.

The Scotsman

Karl Malden and Marlon Brando in *On the Waterfront*

61

DESIRÉE

Directed by Henry Koster   1954

Before Josephine there was Desirée . . . and
some say there was always . . .

Twentieth Century Fox poster

Desirée was adapted from the bestselling
novel by Annemarie Selinko, an authoress
who had clearly done her research in
women's magazines rather than in history
books. Her romantic fiction, about Napoleon
and the love-of-his-life, was a lot of lush
twaddle, a musical comedy without the music.

Great events took place off-screen. The
Battle of Waterloo was merely an entry in
Desirée's diary. The march to Moscow and
the retreat were signalled by flags going in
different directions: bright, clean flags on the
way out; tattered flags on the way back. There
was an edited version of Eugène Delacroix's
famous tableau of Napoleon's coronation.
'Heavens, he's crowned himself!' said
Desirée, just in case anybody hadn't noticed.

Henry Koster's production was very
Hollywooden, painstakingly lavish and utterly
lacking in period feeling. Actors stood round
wearing elegant costumes, in the Directoire
style, straight out of a theatrical wardrobe.

Brando was blamed, unfairly, for the
shortcomings of the film and the superficiality
of his portrait. The performance was
dismissed as monumental miscasting,
ludicrous, quaint, a pseudo-Napoleon in fancy
dress. There were some critics, of course,
who refused to take him seriously in silk and
made easy jokes about *A Streetcar Named
Desirée*. And yet there was a physical
resemblance. He had the intelligence,
authority and, in one moment certainly, as he

Marlon Brando in
Desirée

stood by the mantelpiece brooding in defeat
having just returned from Moscow, he *was*
Napoleon.

Somewhat oddly he adopted an English
accent. 'The situation is desperate,' he said,
parodying one of those frightfully upper-
crust voices. 'That hat doesn't suit you at all.
Do you remember the first night we met?'
Vocally he was so clipped he might have been
playing in Noël Coward's *Private Lives.*

Boney, however, played a decidedly
supporting role to Desirée, known affection-
ately to everybody in the film as Dezzie Ray.
Jean Simmons was very pretty and charming,
even when she was throwing champagne all
over Merle Oberon (in her role as Josephine).
'I'm appalling at learning languages,' she
confessed, having just become a very

reluctant Princess of Sweden. 'May I teach
you your first Swedish word?' replied a tactful
ambassador, attempting to put her at her
ease. And you knew before he said it what the
word was going to be. *Skol.* What else?

The final scene, at Malmaison, took place
on an elegant set of steps, down which cinema
buffs half expected a chorus in white ties and
tails to come dancing and Deanna Durbin to
sing. (Durbin had appeared in many of Henry
Koster's earlier films.) It was here Desirée
managed to persuade Bonaparte to surrender
and save Paris. He handed over his sword to
her. 'Please don't hold it like an umbrella,' he
said. It was a rare moment of wit. Brando
should have appeared in Bernard Shaw's *The
Man of Destiny* instead.

This is probably the worst performance of any star asked to play a character role in costume that Hollywood has ever offered us in a long and dogged assault upon our credulity.

Paul Holt, *Daily Herald*

In my opinion, this is a superb performance, the portait of a great actor just approaching his maturity. I would not have it changed in any detail.

C.A. Lejeune, *Observer*

I know I once said that Marlon Brando is Hollywood's greatest actor, and I am not taking it back. But even great actors can give abysmal, miserable, incompetent, and ludicrous performances.

Leonard Mosley, *Daily Express*

Mr Brando is still the best screen actor in the world, even if on this occasion he has misinterpreted, or been forced to misinterpret, the character he portrays.

Virginia Graham, *Spectator*

It is an interesting performance. Brando has matchless tension and presence as a performer; he is without doubt the most exciting American actor of our day. In *Desirée*, however, he is stiffly posed in every scene, and it must be said that he is seldom more than Marlon Brando in a Napoleon suit.

Lee Rogow, *Saturday Review*

Even in a poor film Brando is incapable of dullness, and his Napoleon is a sketch that contains sufficient substance to make one hope it may one day be expanded to a full portrait.

Fred Majdalany, *Time and Tide*

Jean Simmons and Marlon Brando in *Desirée*

GUYS AND DOLLS

Directed by Joseph L. Mankiewicz   1955

Of all the players this country ever sees there is no doubt that the guy they call Sky is the highest because he goes so high when it comes to betting on any proposition whatsoever he will bet all he has and nobody can bet any more than that.

Damon Runyon, *The Idyll of Miss Sarah Brown*

Guys and Dolls, one of the highwater marks of the American musical theatre, arrived in the wake of the film versions of *Oklahoma!* and *The King and I* and was much preferred; though for those who had seen the New York and London stage productions, the movie was but a pale carbon copy of the original.

There was so much going for the show: a sentimental book which was genuinely funny, lyrics which were witty, music which was pleasant and characters who were engaging. Damon Runyon's pinstripe fairytale, acted with urbane wit and played with blank dice, was a satire on the low life of the small-time crooks who worked in and around Times Square. These bums, broads, pickpockets and touts (gamblers every one of them) were immortalized by their whimsical names and very special line in dialogue.

Nathan Detroit (Frank Sinatra), who ran the oldest established floating crap game in New York and was desperately in need of cash to book a venue, bet Sky Masterson (Marlon Brando) he could not seduce Sergeant Sarah Brown (Jean Simmons) of the Save-a-Soul Mission. Sky, who had a winning way with dolls as well as dice, offered to supply the prudish, all-buttoned-up Sergeant

Marlon Brando and Frank Sinatra in *Guys and Dolls*

with one dozen genuine sinners in exchange for dinner with him in Havana.

Brando had style, authority, charm. All spruced up, smug-elegant in his white suit and black shirt, his jaw jutting in arrogance, he had class. The initial meeting between Sarah and him was beautifully and wittily acted, right through their number, 'I'll Know', and on to the resounding slap in the face. Here was a perfect reminder that, after Somerset Maugham, Frederick Lonsdale and Noël Coward, the comedy of manners had packed her bags and emigrated to America. In a potentially unsympathetic role Brando was surprisingly gentle, surprisingly articulate and surprisingly tender. In fact, he was so delicate with the mission girl that he declined to seduce her, much to her disappointment. 'You're a chump,' she said.

According to the studio's publicity handout, Brando's first reaction on hearing a recording he had made of 'I'll Know' was to say that it sounded to him like the mating call of a yak. Frank Loesser, the composer, was more tactful. 'It's an untrained voice,' he admitted, 'with a pleasing, husky, baritone quality.' The truth was that his singing was barely adequate; certainly his voice had not got the quality to show the songs off to advantage and the gentle huskiness seemed at odds with the character he was playing.

Frank Sinatra acted Nathan as if he wished he were playing Sky. The actors who best epitomized the tawdry-bright cartoon world of Damon Runyon's Broadway were Vivian ('Take Back Your Mink') Blaine and Stubby ('Sit Down You're Rocking The Boat') Kaye. The latter was kept firmly on the

Jean Simmons and Marlon Brando in *Guys and Dolls*

periphery and allowed to rock the boat only *once*. On the New York and London stages he had stopped the show *every* night.

There were no elaborate production numbers. The nearest the film came to choreography was in the cute stylized opening and the crap game in the sewer; but what dancing there was, and it was minimal, merely made one wish Broadway's master choreographer, Michael Kidd, had been allowed to do more.

But Brando is the real surprise. Really for the first time he throws off the mixed-up kid stuff and goes all out with tremendous success to present himself as the great lover loaded with charm.

Jympson Harman, *Evening News*

Marlon Brando, Jean Simmons, Frank Sinatra and Vivian Blaine in *Guys and Dolls*

Mr Brando does very nicely as a musical-comedy hero, but then, once again, he should never do anything nicely. He is a tiger as an actor, and he should behave like a tiger.

The Times

Marlon Brando, as Sky Masterson, is the film's big surprise: his singing is nothing much, but he can play light comedy, and his performance as the gambler – only faintly but still most effectively brooding: a dark-shirted spiv with a whiff of Hamlet about him – is a delight.

Isabel Quigly, *Spectator*

Brando, looking slightly in pain, gets his songs over in the Gene Kelly style: wobbling a bit, but full of charm. He picks his way through Frank Loesser's lyrics with the skill of a sapper in a minefield, gingerly confident.

Anthony Carthew, *Daily Herald*

Mr Brando proves that he can be polite and articulate.

Manchester Guardian

THE TEAHOUSE OF THE AUGUST MOON

Directed by Daniel Mann   1956

The Teahouse of the August Moon was a satire on US policy in the Far East. In seeking to westernize the natives, the American army themselves became orientalized. The conquerers were conquered.

John Patrick's stage comedy (based on Vern Sneider's novel) always had been very thin. The fun was of the simplest kind and might have served as the basis for a musical.

Transferred to television it might have done for a one half-hour episode in a sitcom series. But transferred to cinemascope, practically intact, and just plonked on the screen, the satire was so gentle that it disappeared up its own sentimentality. The film, heavy-handed, over-long and over-faithful to the Broadway original, got better notices than it deserved.

Brando was cast as Sakini, a lazy but wily

Marlon Brando and Glenn Ford in *The Teahouse of the August Moon*

interpreter, who also acted as Greek chorus. He had a long opening monologue, played straight into the camera, which was ponderous in its moralizing and difficult to follow. It seemed as if his mouth had been stuffed with an extra set of teeth and lumps of cotton wool. He was at his funniest when he pretended to wake from a deep sleep and kicked his legs out at lightning speed.

Brando's make-up was quite extraordinary; yet the moment he was put among the natives, he quite clearly was not the genuine article. However, if Brando always looked like an actor made up, the natives looked exactly what they were: hired-on-the-spot farmers and children, who had never appeared in front of a camera in their lives. Even the professionals among them behaved like amateurs, mugging away in a manner which should never have been countenanced.

Brando got star billing, but was, in fact, playing a supporting and unrewarding role to Glenn Ford. Ford had infinitely more charm and was certainly far more humorous as the bewildered and well-meaning young captain who, having been posted to the village of Tobiko to build a Pentagon-shaped schoolhouse, went all native and built a teahouse for the geisha girls instead.

Paul Ford, re-creating his stage role of the blustering, deskbound Colonel Purdey, was splendid. 'They're gonna learn democracy,' he said, 'if I've gotta shoot everyone of them!' Ironically, Ford had only landed the part when Louis Calherne died in the middle of the production.

The film was shot on location but for all cinemagoers saw of Okinawania, MGM might

just as well have stayed in its own backyard. As things turned out, it rained so much they had to come home anyway and complete the movie in Hollywood.

Glenn Ford and Marlon Brando in *The Teahouse of the August Moon*

Like Olivier, Brando has both the talent and the willingness to submerge himself with zest into improbable parts and if this is unlikely to be his most remembered performance it is still amusing and to his credit that he did it at all.

Fred Majdalany, *Time and Tide*

The highly talented Marlon Brando is virtually wasted as the artificial young Okinawan.

Hollis Alpert, *Saturday Review*

It is a clever performance up to a point, but it might be admitted that his Okinawan manner, once adopted, does not permit much variation.

Sydney Morning Herald

Machiko Kyo, Marlon Brando and Glenn Ford in *The Teahouse of the August Moon*

73

SAYONARA

Directed by Joshua Logan   1957

Marlon Brando was cast as Major Lloyd Gruver, an ace hero suffering from combat fatigue in the Korean War, who was sent to Japan to recuperate; but instead of spending time with his fiancée, a general's daughter, he fell in love with a Japanese dancer (Miiko Taka) and went all Japanese.

The American armed forces disapproved of mixed marriages and did everything they could to make life difficult for servicemen who did marry, even to making it illegal for them to take their wives back to the United States and then posting the men home, claiming that was what most of them wanted.

Sayonara was a plea for greater racial toleration; but long before the film had been released, the law had been changed. Joshua Logan's treatment of its subject matter was soft-centred and facile, while the actual look of the production never rose above a pretty-postcard level, with endless and unimaginative shots of pretty girls crossing pretty bridges. There were tantalizing glimpses of the Kabuki Theatre, starring Ricardo Montalban. (Why Montalban? Were there no Kabuki actors available to play the part?) There were also extracts from the Bunraku Puppet Theatre and the Matsubayashi all-girl show, a production which owed more to Broadway than it did to the East and whose extracts were so brief as to be no more than a trailer.

Major Gruver, a Texan by birth, disapproved strongly of his friend Kelly (Red Buttons) marrying a Japanese girl (Miyoshi Umeki) until he himself fell in love. The role thereafter did not require Brando to do much more than to be gentle and tender and this he did with considerable charm and a big, winning smile. His best moments were when he was observed considering what his fiancée and her father would have to say about his forthcoming marriage to a Japanese girl.

The performance had a quiet strength throughout. It was typical of Brando that the opening shot of him, sitting in the cockpit, should manage to convey his attitude to the war without any words whatsoever. Similarly, Gruver's rebellion against officialdom and prejudice was acted without histrionics; even his one potentially big dramatic scene (the discovery of the mutual suicide of Kelly and his wife) was under-played.

The slushy happy ending (evidently, insisted on by Brando), in which he married the dancer, was awfully glib and unconvincing. In the novel the lovers had parted. Hence, the title. In the film the press eagerly asked the major what his message was for the world. 'Tell them we said "sayonara",' he replied, 'sayonara' now meaning 'goodbye' to Japan and the big brass, who had wanted to stop the marriage.

The *Madam Butterfly* bit of the story was restricted to the sub-plot. Actually, the sub-plot, with Kelly being willing to waive all his legal rights in order to marry a Japanese girl, was not only more interesting, it was also more poignant, not least because Miyoshi Umeki was a better actress than the inexperienced Miiko Taka. Taka, in her white sweater, white slacks, white hat and white make-up, was so artificial she might have been appearing in drag in a number from her stage show.

Miiko Taka and Marlon Brando in *Sayonara*

75

The atmosphere of oriental tranquillity which Mr Logan builds up is heightened by Mr Brando in the part of this quiet, unhurried American. It is a performance of deceptive talent – a performance which grows in sympathy and understanding as the film progresses until it is fully realised; but script, dialogue and direction also play their part in building up a character who will not easily be forgotten.

The Times

There is always the fascination in watching him play a routine scene, with no special dramatic depth, and observing the authority with which he imposes himself and controls his effects. Without a great deal of assistance, he gives this over-weighted film such strength as it has.

John Cutts, *Sight and Sound*

But Mr Brando's Southern accent, imposed upon a Method mumble, makes nine-tenths of what he has to say incomprehensible to a foreign listener. Perhaps sub-titles would help him to be understood.

C.A. Lejeune, *Observer*

The Method, even in these cherry-blossom surroundings, is fascinating; but one wishes him better, and briefer, luck next time.

William Whitebait, *New Statesman*

Joshua Logan, Marlon Brando and William Goetz greeted with flowers during the filming of *Sayonara*

The comedian Red Buttons was excellent in his first straight role and he and Umeki won Oscars for the best supporting actor and actress. Brando was also nominated, but lost out to Alec Guinness in *The Bridge on the River Kwai*.

Miiko Taka and Marlon Brando in *Sayonara*

THE YOUNG LIONS

Directed by Edward Dmytryk   1958

The Young Lions was based on Irwin Shaw's bestseller and described three servicemen's experiences during World War II. The singer Dean Martin, in his first straight role, played a cowardly Broadway star trying to dodge service. A very haggard and very earnest Montgomery Clift played a baited American Jew, who was so fragile he looked as if he might break at any moment. Brando was cast as Christian Diestl, a young ski instructor turned Wehrmacht officer, loyal to Germany and totally ignorant of the atrocities of the Nazis. Diestl genuinely believed Hitler and National Socialism would bring peace and prosperity to the world.

In his peak cap, grey riding breeches, jackboots, plus his Iron Cross and polite manners, Brando always cut a proud, dignified and romantic figure, whether he was eating a snowball, fraternizing with the French or sleeping with his commanding officer's wife (May Britt). His German accent tended to put everybody else's German accent to shame.

His subtle, thoughtful performance (so thoughtful he might have sat for Auguste Rodin) caught the bewilderment of a man torn between his dedicated patriotism and his essential humanitarianism and decency. It was a performance of restrained power.

The Young Lions was essentially a propaganda piece. Ever mindful of the American and German box offices, the scriptwriters had toned down the anti-semitism and also toned down the brutality of the Nazi to make Diestl a more sympathetic character. By doing so, the studio ended up with something much

Marlon Brando in
The Young Lions

78

more superficial than, perhaps, they had intended.

Those who had read Irwin Shaw's novel found Brando's sensitive performance far too humane and objected strongly that a ruthless killer had been turned into a disillusioned idealist. Every scene in which Diestl appeared was there to establish the good German. 'Be nice to him,' said one French woman to another, 'he's the best of the best.'

In the novel, Diestl was a sergeant consenting to Nazism; in the film Diestl was a lieutenant reluctantly acquiescing. Exposed to SS brutality, Diestl immediately asked for a transfer. Behind the British lines in North Africa (the most graphic scene in the film), he refused to shoot wounded and blinded soldiers caught in a deadly ambush.

Diestl's sentimentality, morality and individualism were not appreciated by his commanding officer, Captain Hardenberg (Maximilian Schell), who believed the German army was invincible only because it obeyed any order, however distasteful. Their exchanges tended towards melodrama. 'I am sick of doing my duty,' said Diestl, as they made their escape on a motorbike, roaring across the desert. 'Men like you poison the army. I should have shot you,' said Hardenberg. 'Why didn't you shoot me then?' asked Diestl. 'Because I was an idiot,' replied Hardenberg.

Their conversation was cut short by a mine. Hardenberg ended up in hospital, his face totally covered in bandages with only a tiny slit near his mouth. Looking unfortunately somewhat comic, he asked Diestl for a bayonet so that he could put the chap in the

Marlon Brando and May Britt in *The Young Lions*

next bed out of his misery. Diestl seemed surprised to learn later that Hardenberg had killed himself.

In the novel, the sergeant killed a French boy in order to steal his bicycle. In the film, the lieutenant looked with the deepest compassion on a crippled lad, hobbling through the ruins of the city. Finally, sickened by what he had seen in a concentration camp, Diestl staggered into the countryside,

Marlon Brando in
The Young Lions

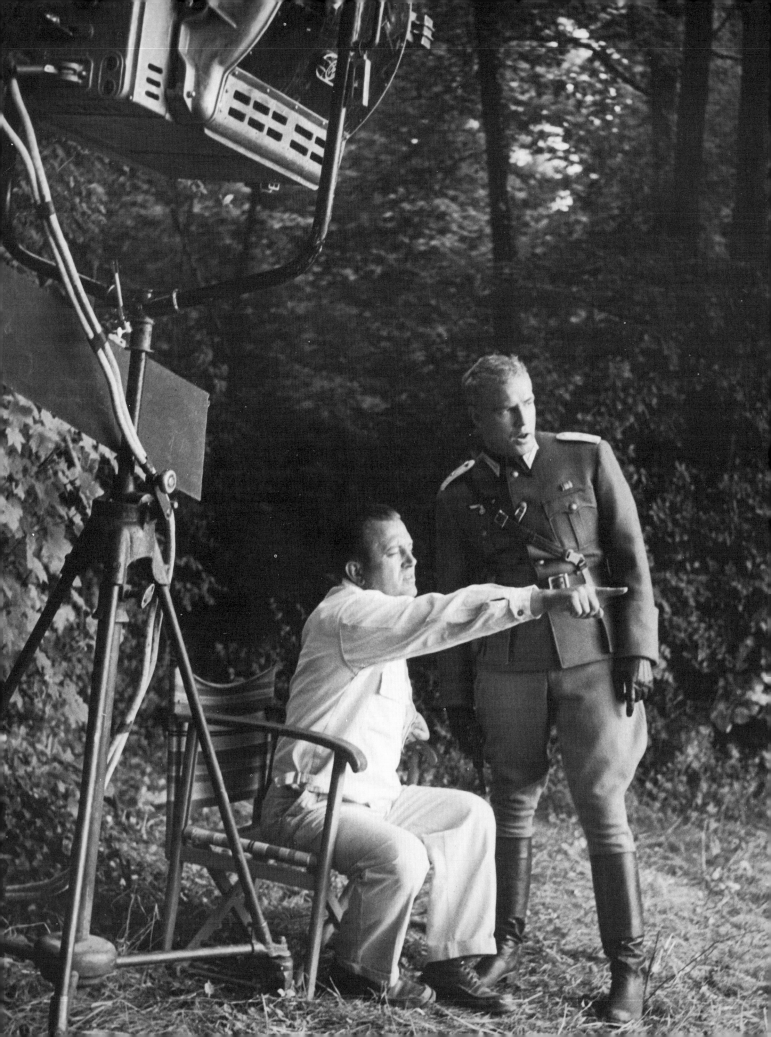

smashed his gun on a tree stump and decided he would fight no longer. Seconds later he was shot dead by the Dean Martin character – the two separate stories meeting head-on, for the first time, in a stagey climax.

The credit for turning a third-rate best seller into a second-rate box office hit undoubtedly rests with Marlon Brando. If anything can make one believe in the cardboard carnage it is his magnificent vitality, as he struts broodingly through the wreckage. He sometimes overdoes it to the extent of looking as if his head was permanently trapped in a 'think' bubble, but before his hypnotic presence one merely notes this as a stylistic arabesque.

David Watts, *Financial Times*

It may be argued in defence of *The Young Lions* that Mr Marlon Brando, in the part of the young German who glories in his country's strength, is helping to expose the evil belief that might is right; but Mr Brando fails altogether to carry through with his portrait, for here is no suggestion of Aryan despotism or jackboot arrogance. Instead we encounter only an honourable perplexity over the conflicting impulses of patriotism and humanitarianism.

The Times

Marlon Brando, as always, is impressive and dynamic in his odd way; his is an achievement of personality rather than impersonation.

Manchester Guardian

To me, Brando is always fascinating to watch. Like other American actors who understand the tremendous expressive revelation of the camera lens (such as Cagney, Ferrer, Bogart, Lee Cobb, Fonda and, more recently, Cassavetes and Franciosa), Brando's mere presence on the screen is dynamic and compelling. And he knows it! Coiled like a spring, he brings a powerful impact to the young lieutenant.

Paul Rotha, *Films and Filming*

Marlon Brando and
Maximilian Schell in
The Young Lions

Edward Dmytryk and
Marlon Brando filming
The Young Lions

The 1960s

Marlon Brando in
One-Eyed Jacks

THE FUGITIVE KIND

Directed by Sidney Lumet   1960

They say a woman can burn a man down, but I can burn a woman down.

Val Xavier

Battle of Angels, an early Tennessee Williams drama and a favourite with the playwright, opened and closed out of town in 1939. Williams rewrote it and it was produced on Broadway in 1957 as *Orpheus Descending*. Three years later it appeared on the big screen as *The Fugitive Kind*. He went on rewriting the play, off and on, for the rest of his life.

Williams described the play as the story of a wild, spirited boy who wandered into the conventional community of the South and created the commotion of a fox in a chicken coop. The commotion was so operatic that some theatregoers would not have been surprised had the actors started singing. In the cinema, even though the poetry, the arias and the atmospheric music had all been jettisoned, Sidney Lumet's production still remained very stagey.

The action was set in the general store in Two Rivers, a small Mississippi town, a modern Hell. The store was run by Lady Torrance, a middle-aged Eurydice, lonely and sex-starved, who was drawn back to life by a modern Orpheus, Val Xavier, a handsome, itinerant café-entertainer, who had recently been run out of New Orleans. 'You're not young at 30,' he observed, 'if you've been at a party since you were 15 . . .'

Xavier had lived with corruption all his life and yet had managed, somehow, to have come through all his experiences uncorrupted.

Anna Magnani and Marlon Brando in *The Fugitive Kind*

He sported a snakeskin jacket and carried a guitar, symbols of his freedom and sensuality. Xavier, however, was not responsible for the dangerous potency of his sex appeal; he would have liked nothing better than a steady job and to have been left alone.

Lady employed him as a shop salesman by day and as a stud by night. The story ended in an extravagant and melodramatic fashion when she, pregnant by him, was shot by her evil husband, who then set fire to the store. It will be remembered that in the legend, Orpheus was torn to pieces by harpies. In the play, Xavier was torn to pieces by the sheriff's dogs; in the film, he was driven back into the flames by the sheriff's men with water-hoses. Finally, all that was left of him was his skin jacket. Wild things, we were told, leave skins behind so that the fugitive kind can always find their own kind.

Brando was beautifully controlled; though every so often, as might be expected, the violence would erupt on a line like 'Who are you calling cheap?' The one poetic passage which had been preserved, that extraordinary description of birds without wings and legs, was eloquently delivered. There was also a marvellous pre-credit sequence (for many, the highlight of the film) when Xavier was on a charge of having broken up a joint in New Orleans and described his life, straight to the camera. The monologue was specially written for the film and does not appear in the play. Brando's expressive eyes conveyed his innermost thoughts.

Lady was played by Anna Magnani, the Italian actress, who was never afraid of the

Anna Magnani,
Marlon Brando and
Joanne Woodward in
The Fugitive Kind

big effect. The drama became not so much a
duel of angels, said the wags, as a clash of
egos. Magnani was even more difficult to
understand than Brando. (There were those
who thought the film should have had
subtitles.) But the great weakness of the
casting was that it was difficult to believe that
these two particular people actually loved
each other.

Joanne Woodward played a rich, wild and
exhibitionistic nymphomaniac-dipsomaniac,
all washed up by corruption. With white
make-up, black eyes and bleeding nose,
Woodward had a great time showing
everybody just how lewd a lewd vagrant could
be if she tried hard enough. 'I want something to hold the way you hold your guitar,'
she said, kneeling before Xavier and making
it very clear that whatever it was that she

Marlon Brando and
Victor Jory in
The Fugitive Kind

wanted to hold, she was going to hold it in her
mouth.

Victor Jory was well cast as Lady's
venomous, cancerous husband, a powerful
and frightening portrait of a dying man
refusing to go quietly into the dark night.

**The Great Love between them never gets much
further than Great Acting.**

William Whitebait, *New Statesmen and Nation*

**Brando has it all ways – youth and agelessness,
looks that can quite properly be called 'legendary'
because they are, as it were, an incarnation of all
sorts of legends, ancient and modern; all of which
rather clouds his performance, which here seems
little but laboured, conscientious and (all ways)
methodical.**

Isabel Quigly, *Spectator*

**In general, though, Brando gives an uncannily
affecting performance, and what affects the
audience is not his acting – he passionately refuses
to act – but his own luminous, personal intensity.**

Time Magazine

**Watching Brando imitating Judy Holliday's
impersonation of him in *Bells Are Ringing* is, at its
most serious, like seeing a scratchy old film of
Duse or Bernhardt; surely someone is kidding
someone?**

Clancy Sigal, *Time and Tide*

ONE-EYED JACKS

Directed by Marlon Brando   1961

I have the obligation and the opportunity in a recently discovered impulse to try to communicate the things I think are important. I want to make a frontal assault on the temple of clichés.

Our early-day heroes were not brave one hundred per cent nor were they good one hundred per cent of the time. My part is that of a man who is intuitive and suspicious, proud and searching. He has a touch of the vain and a childish and disproportionate sense of virtue and manly ethics. He is lonely and generally distrustful of human contacts. Properly handled, the folklore of the outdoor era contains all the vital ingredients of powerful picture-making.

Marlon Brando

Pina Pellicier and Marlon Brando in *One-Eyed Jacks*

The critics did not take kindly to the pretentious publicity and Brando himself was stupid enough to dismiss *One-Eyed Jacks* as a pot-boiler. Over the years, the film's reputation, however, has continued to grow and it is now much better received than it was in its day.

The script was a classic Western melodrama of betrayal and revenge, which owed something to the Billy the Kid and Pat Garrett legend. Brando and Karl Malden played Rio and Dad Longworth, partners in crime. The story began with a raid on a bank followed by a visit to a brothel, both carried out in high spirits, which led to a dusty chase across the dunes, ending with the older man betraying the younger to the forces of the law.

Longworth became a much respected sheriff while Rio languished in prison, incapable of forgetting Dad's desertion and treachery. 'He was the best friend I ever had. He left me rot – and you know what for? For two sacks of gold.' Six years later he escaped and his first act of revenge was to seduce Longworth's daughter (a performance of great beauty and delicacy by Pina Pellicier).

There was a memorable composition of Dad lying horizontal on the verandah of his house at the very front of the frame. The verandah's fencing cut the frame in two and in the far distance could be seen an advancing horseman, whom Longworth instinctively knew was Rio.

Marlon Brando in
One-Eyed Jacks

The reunion of the two men, sizing each other up, lying to each other, was excellent poker. 'You're a one-eyed Jack round here, Dad,' said Rio. 'I seen the other side of your face.' Actually both men were one-eyed Jacks, showing only one side of their faces to the rest of the pack. The key difference was that Rio, who was essentially honest, showed only his bad side, while the sheriff, who was essentially evil, showed only his good side.

Asked by Longworth to hand over his gun, there was a close-up of Brando's enigmatic face, and just in case cinemagoers should fail to recognize just how enigmatic his face was, there was a painting of the Mona Lisa hanging in the saloon bar. 'Let's see the kind of stuff you are made of,' said the sheriff, giving Rio a vicious public flogging, far worse than anything Terry Malone had suffered on the waterfront. 'You better kill me,' warned Rio. But snarling villains never do kill the hero when they have the opportunity to do so. The sheriff, mistakenly, thought it was enough to smash the kid's gun hand to pulp. There was a shot later of Rio lying in agony on his bed which would have had the great French painter, David, running for a new canvas.

There was an excellent scene in prison. Karl Malden, with his wicked eyes and his wicked moustache, was evil writ very large. Dad was a mordant, ruthless, vindictive hypocrite. 'Oh, sure, kid, you'll get a fair trial and then I'm going to hang you personally.'

The two actors played off each other. The final shoot-out in the town square, round the fountain, was a characteristic exposure of the Western myth, ending with the hero shooting the villain in the back.

Karl Malden and Marlon Brando in *One-Eyed Jacks*

Brando, though he exerted, as usual, his extraordinary physical power and presence, was far too old to be playing Kid to Malden's Dad. In his yellow straw sombrero and heavy red-striped serape, he cut a negative and occasionally comic figure. There were too many dead looks, too many pregnant pauses, too much reliance on improvisation, too many awkward close-ups of his sullen face registering absolutely nothing. He was at times, almost a parody of a miserable, mumbling cowboy.

The action was realistic, but the locations were romantic and Charles Lang Jr's lyrical photography of Death Valley and the Californian coastline near Monterey was breathtaking.

Director Brando, however, comes off much better than Actor Brando, the Method Cowboy, who incessantly mumbles, scratches, blinks, rubs his nose and sulks. In short, Brando plays the same character he always plays, the only character who seems to interest him: Marlon Brando. A childish thing indeed.

Time Magazine

As to Brando himself, the prototype, it is hard to resist a feeling that success was often in spite of, rather than because of, his loyalty to The Method. While his worst habits – the monotony, the excessive cultivation of inarticulateness – can often be traced to a conscious but imperfect application of The Method; his best qualities – his energy and the emotive power – are innate, patently unschooled and uncultivated.

David Robinson, *Financial Times*

Karl Malden,
Marlon Brando and
Slim Pickens in
One-Eyed Jacks

Mr Brando is today probably the most imitated actor in films. In *One-Eyed Jacks* he is imitating himself – and in a manner that comes close to parody.

Thomas Wiseman, *Sunday Express*

He has provided an object lesson in the unwisdom of trying to be star and director of one and the same film: for the director has here shown a ruinous lack of severity in curbing the star's repetitive idiosyncrasies. He has given us a quite indigestible dose of Mr Brando's flat, laconic utterances.

Guardian

Brando is less an actor than a presence, one of those Archetypical Figures that correspond to some basic requirement of the times. Will people in thirty years find him ludicrous – slouch, mumble, pregnant silences, dazzling though heavy looks, lowering gait, oppressiveness and all? His personality is so much at home in the present that in films he can hardly go wrong. The parts he is given may not always be up to much but he gets over that; from start to finish he appears to be playing himself, with the limitations and the advantages that implies.

Isabel Quigly, *Spectator*

MUTINY ON THE BOUNTY

Directed by Lewis Milestone   1962

1962 was the year of the cat o' nine tails, with cinemas showing no less than three naval yarns, all set on the high seas in the late eighteenth century. They included *Billy Budd* with Peter Ustinov, Robert Ryan and Terence Stamp, *HMS Defiant* with Alec Guinness and Dirk Bogarde, and a remake of the Oscar-winning 1935 *Mutiny on the Bounty* with Marlon Brando and Trevor Howard in the roles originally played by Clark Gable and the unforgettable Charles Laughton.

Captain Bligh (Trevor Howard) was sent by the Admiralty to obtain samples of the breadfruit plant from the island of Tahiti. He was a strict disciplinarian, a two-dozen-lash man, who always put the mission first and the lives of the men second. Fear was the best weapon, he said. It was the offer of a mere ladleful of water to a dying man which finally sparked off the mutiny.

The antagonism between Bligh and Christian (Marlon Brando) was not just a clash of

Lisa Simone, Trevor Howard, Marlon Brando and Antoinette Bower in *Mutiny on the Bounty*

personalities. It was a social clash. As far as Christian and the Admiralty were concerned, Bligh was not a gentleman. Christian was portrayed as an upper-class dandy, formally polite, superciliously rude and very much the ladies' man, who arrived at the quayside with two floozies in tow. Later he was seen sitting in his cabin, wearing a quilted dressing-gown and a silk nightcap, smoking a pipe.

Brando was quite capable of suggesting beneath the peacock façade the decent, humane, introspective officer with a social conscience. Unfortunately, since the script never developed his relationship with the mutineers (led by Richard Harris), he had to do this without the benefit of dialogue. What dialogue there was tended to get in the way of his performance.

Christian had a nice line in insolent wit with a smile: 'I assure you, sir,' he said to Bligh, 'that the execution of my duties is entirely unaffected by my personal attitude to you.' There was also always the pleasure of the jokey and patronizing la-di-da accent. 'Oh, isn't this jolly,' he remarked, putting on a native head-dress. 'You are amused,' said Bligh when he was forced to dance. 'I hope I shall not be,' replied Christian. Ordered by Bligh to make love to the chieftain's daughter (Tarita), he inquired: 'Is that an order, sir? Might I have it entered in the log? I'll try my best.' And off he went to rub noses to the tune of 'Rule Britannia'. Vocally, Brando was very funny and the confrontations were always highly entertaining.

What the film showed, once Bligh had been overthrown, was pure fiction. There was an ill-thought out speech by Christian about

returning home and facing court martial, which led to the burning of the *Bounty* by three members of the crew, who were not keen to be hanged. Christian, in attempting to put out the flames and save the sextant, sustained terrible burns. This was then followed by a protracted death scene, badly acted, accompanied by close-ups of a tearful girlfriend and sincere apologies from the crew; and, as if all this were not enough, there was also a heavenly choir on the soundtrack. 'What a useless way to die,' observed Christian, understandably morose. It was a dreadful anti-climax. What had actually happened on Pitcairn Island was far more dramatic and exciting. The mutineers had run amok, killing the islanders and themselves. Christian was murdered.

The critics were divided as to which actor gave the best performance. Trevor Howard, first-rate, managed to convey the loneliness of command beneath the unsmiling, granite-like features; he was far less theatrical and far more sympathetic than Charles Laughton had been. However, there could never be any doubt that, in this version, Christian was the leading role, scripted and acted so as always to upstage Bligh. There was a typical moment when Christian had to tell him his cabin was awash and offered his insincere sympathy.

The idyllic Tahitian interlude was the stuff of which overlong travelogues are made, mere window-dressing, and much nearer to Dorothy Lamour than anything else. The fishing, and especially the dancing, was just the sort of thing the British royal family has to sit through on their travels abroad; though why the editor should think cinemagoers

96

wanted to look at the girls' faces during the hula-hula was not clear. By way of compensation the screen offered occasional close-ups of phallic bananas and wilting breadfruit.

Robert L. Surtees' colour photography was handsome, doing justice to the lyrical and storm passages. There were some magnificent seascapes with the *Bounty* in full sail. The ship was undoubtedly the star turn and physically more convincing than the crew, which included such stalwart hands as Hugh Griffith, Percy Herbert, Gordon Jackson, Chips Rafferty – and not a decent part between them.

Both actors give towering performances and it doesn't whittle a chip off Trevor Howard's if I say right away that Brando, who takes the most colossal risk, brings the more showy skill to bear.

Alexander Walker, *Evening Standard*

It is a duel in which Mr Brando is handicapped, partly by accent, partly by his very distinctive appearance, which never really seems to belong to a British naval officer of the eighteenth century or any other century. Nevertheless, Mr Brando, by force simply of his very strong personality, makes a good fight of it. Between him and the more natural seeming Mr Howard, honours may not be quite even, but they are even enough to maintain dramatic tension.

Guardian

Mr Brando is postively exquisite . . . one adjective I never thought would be applicable to him.

Thomas Wiseman, *Sunday Express*

Tarita and Marlon Brando in *Mutiny on the Bounty*

THE
UGLY AMERICAN

Directed by George Englund   1963

Democracy is a farce. It's for white people only.

Harrison Carter MacWhite

The Ugly American opened with a disclaimer to the effect that, though it had been shot in Thailand, it did not reflect the politics and history of Thailand.

The film was a caustic and candid account of the hamfisted way the US conducted her foreign policy by warmongering, supporting dictators and sacrificing principles for expediency. The message was quite clear: that if America was to win the Cold War, she had to remember what she was fighting for as well as what she was against. Nationalism, populism, anti-Americanism did not necessarily imply communism, and democracy could only suffer by her branding all that she hated and feared as communist.

Harrison Carter MacWhite, a vigorous young diplomat, designated ambassador to South Sarkham (a mythical country in South-East Asia), arrived in the capital, determined to save the country from the Reds. South Sarkham had a dictator backed by the US, while North Sarkham was communist. Never for a moment doubting the rightness of his mission, MacWhite mistook a popular leader's nationalism for communism and unintentionally sparked off a civil war.

The key scene was a drunken slanging match during which the ambassador realized he had misjudged the revolutionary hero. The man, a former wartime buddy, was, in fact, a dupe of the communists. The dialogue, heavy-

going, artificial and awkwardly edited, was further hampered by Japanese actor Eija Okada's diction. Okada, who had starred in the highly successful *Hiroshima, Mon Amour*, had great difficulty in speaking in English.

Brando looked the diplomat. He wore horn-rimmed spectacles, sported a Ronald Colman moustache and smoked a briar pipe. At one point, he appeared in top hat and frockcoat, producing audible gasps of amazement from cinemagoers. There was an excellent scene when MacWhite was being cross-examined by the senators in Washington. His dignity was totally unassailable.

The Ugly American was a serious film about a serious problem, satirizing the indifference of America very neatly when the ambassador was back in the US, speaking on TV and about

Arthur Hill, Frances Helm and Marlon Brando in *The Ugly American*

Kukrit Pramoj, Arthur Hill and Marlon Brando in *The Ugly American*

101

Eija Okada and
Marlon Brando in
The Ugly American

to make the main point in his speech. 'What the American people must realize now,' he began; he got no further for even as he was saying it the hand of an unseen person switched off the television set.

Kukrit Pramoj, witty and camp as the corrupt Prime Minister, gave a very smooth performance indeed.

It is the most restrained and, in its way, the most brilliant performance of his career.

Leonard Mosley, *Daily Express*

It would be an utterly banal film if it were not for Brando.

Alexander Walker, *Evening Standard*

Marlon Brando gives his best performance in years. . . . Caricature is avoided; the portrait is observed minutely, and entirely without malice.

Philip Oakes, *Sunday Telegraph*

Mr Brando stays rather subdued throughout, though at least even at his dullest he looks and acts every inch a star.

The Times

I'd go a hundred miles to see him as Mickey Mouse. Unfortunately that's about all this film amounts to.

Penelope Gilliatt, *Observer*

102

BEDTIME STORY

Directed by Ralph Levy   1964

Jamison: Is there a name for men who get
money from women?
Benson: Yes, smart.

Though made in the 1960s, *Bedtime Story* was
a typical 1930s comedy about a pair of
confidence tricksters, ace seducers, fleecing
rich and silly women on the French Riviera.
The pleasure of the movie came from
watching the two adventurers outwitting each
other in a series of moves and counter-
manoeuvres, double- and treble-crossing
each other.

David Niven was cast as Lawrence Jamison,
the big operator, pretending to be an exiled
Prince raising money for his people. Jamison
was a lion among conmen, king of the
mountain. He was romantic, elegant,
debonair, a man of the world, suave, cultured,
intelligent, well-bred. In short, David Niven
effortlessly projected David Niven's favourite
screen persona, himself, with immense style,
charm, economy and subtlety.

Marlon Brando was Fred Benson, the
smalltime operator, an ex-army corporal, who
spun a line about his ailing and highly
fictitious grandmother. Benson was not so
much a lion, as a cute wolf and his little Red
Riding Hoods were quickly disarmed by his
hard-luck story and his charming, little-boy
smile. They were soon parted from their
money and other disposables. There was a
moment when Benson was caught with his
pants down but all sex took place off-screen.

The lion and the wolf formed an unlikely
partnership, which worked perfectly well
until they became rivals for the affections of a

girl (Shirley Jones), whom they believed to be
a millionaire's daughter, a soap heiress.

Benson was disguised at one stage as a
mentally defective Ruritanian Hapsburg, who
behaved like an animal and had to be fed at
table. Brando's elephantine behaviour was
crude and self-indulgent yet undeniably funny
when he was rummaging in a silly little purse
and addressing all Jamison's conquests as
'Mother'. Later, Benson posed as a
wheelchair paraplegic to gain the heiress's
sympathy, only to find himself at a receiving
end of a sound thrashing by Jamison and
unable to express the excrutiating pain he was
feeling. There were those who found Brando's
caricature of his role in *The Men* in bad taste.

Shirley Jones and
Marlon Brando in
Bedtime Story

David Niven and
Marlon Brando in
Bedtime Story

Many critics took the comedy far too seriously. The script's main fault was not its bad taste but its happy ending when it was revealed that Jamison was immensely philanthropic and Benson was seen to reform and marry the heroine. The film should have had the courage not to compromise. The true happy ending (and highly moral), surely, would have been to reveal that the soap heiress was also a confidence trickster and had rooked them. And this is what happened when Hollywood remade the film twenty-four years later in the inferior *Dirty Rotten Scoundrels*, with Michael Caine and Steve Martin miscast in the Niven and Brando roles.

Comedies such as this utilize for their humour a kind of unconsummated pornographic approach we know to be sure fire on the American market. Twenty or thirty years from now a new generation may look back on these Shapiro-type movies of the Sixties and find them charming in their old-fashioned nostalgia.

Hollis Alpert, *Saturday Review*

The wake of the history of the cinema is scattered with bubbling noxious garbage, for there is nothing else in art or entertainment that can quite equal the stink of a can of commercial film that has had the microbes at it, but I don't remember a movie like this for a long time. It makes you feel that civilisation might as well leave it to the amoebae again.

Penelope Gilliatt, *Observer*

Marlon Brando in
Bedtime Story

THE SABOTEUR:
CODE NAME 'MORITURI'

Directed by Bernhard Wicki   1965

Morituri te salutant (Those who are about to die salute you)

Roman gladiators' salute to Caesar

The film began life as *Morituri*. The title was changed to *Code Name: Morituri* and then changed, yet again, this time to *The Saboteur: Code Name 'Morituri'*. The lengthening of the title did nothing to improve the film and the critics treated this World War II sea drama in much the same manner as the Caesars had treated the gladiators. They gave it the thumbs-down.

The story was set on board a German merchant-ship sailing from Japan to Bordeaux with a cargo of 7,000 tons of raw rubber, which the Allies wanted to intercept and capture. The screenplay, unbelievable and silly, was often so incoherent and inconclusive as to suggest that much of the film had been left on the cutting-room floor. There were clearly intentions, *en passant*, to make some serious political statements on war – good Germans, bad Germans, persecuted Jews, British moral degeneracy, American gang rape; but none of these things were properly focused and the characters' motivations were often obscure and always melodramatic.

A German engineer (Marlon Brando), an anti-Nazi and a pacifist, convinced all wars were idiotic and that they solved nothing, had fled Germany rather than go to the Russian front. He preferred to live the good life in India with his books, music, modest art collection and a beautiful lady from time to time, valuing his privacy most of all.

There was a good scene right at the beginning when Trevor Howard (in his guest-star role of British Intelligence Officer) blackmailed the engineer into posing as a top-ranking member of the SS and dismantling the scuttling charges on the freighter. 'You will be arrogant, brutal, rude and conceited – shouldn't be difficult for you.' The scene had an appealing irony. 'You're a cold bastard,' said the engineer. 'I live on a chilly island,' replied the Brit.

There was some tension when Brando (in good physical shape) was creeping about the smoky hull among the girders and pistons, climbing steel ladders and dismantling the charges. The noise of the engines made a far better and certainly a more exciting soundtrack than Jerry Goldsmith's score.

A notable feature of the role was the way it allowed Brando to play both the good and the bad German. The good German's credentials were established when he took his rage and exasperation out on a poor defenceless bookshelf. The German accent, as usual, was impeccable. He was more German than the German actors and the accent was used for maximum comic effect. There was an amusing scene when the First Officer (Martin Benrath), a dedicated yet very gullible member of the Nazi Party, was being flattered. 'You are a genuine German in the best sense of the phrase.' The inflection was spot on. There were times, however, when the diction was so very precise that audiences had the feeling Brando was sending up the script.

The people who wrote the copy for the poster had clearly not seen the film. *The*

Trevor Howard and Marlon Brando in *The Saboteur: Code Name 'Morituri'*

107

Yul Brynner, Janet Margolin, Wally Cox and Marlon Brando in *The Saboteur: Code Name 'Morituri'*

Janet Margolin and Marlon Brando in *The Saboteur: Code Name 'Morituri'*

Marlon Brando, it must be admitted, presents in *Morituri* the most interesting and persuasive performance he has delivered in years.

Arthur Knight, *Saturday Review*

Instead of playing a man he plays an accent, a German accent full of lisps and hisses, an accent far more amusing than anything Peter Sellers developed in *Dr Strangelove*. Brando owes himself and his art more than this. He is a phenomenally talented man. He is interesting even when he is being ridiculous. He has his pick of directors and scripts; he can make a picture as he pleases. Yet he contents himself with patent claptrap like *Morituri*.

Newsweek

Brando shows his true quality for the first time in a decade, with a perfect German accent, a silky smile, a flair for deadpan ironic comedy and miraculous timing that explains every pause and hesitation as exhaustively as a footnote. Outside the masterworks, one seldom encounters screen acting as subtle as this.

Kenneth Tynan, *Observer*

Brando, staring through his nose and chopping his pauses into personalised fragments, is as impressive as ever, but the only roots a movie like this recognises lead straight to the bank.

John Coleman, *New Statesman*

As one who has spent a good many years in Germany, I can testify that Brando's portrayal of a citizen of the Reich is brilliant characterisation down to the last umlaut.

Leonard Mosley, *Daily Express*

unleashed power of Marlon Brando . . . the raging fury of Yul Brynner . . . Now for the first time these two great actors clash . . . their battleground the Seven Seas. None of this appeared in the film. Brando and Brynner often seemed, in fact, to be in different films, each going his separate way.

Brynner (who made no attempt at a German accent) played the decent and humane captain of the merchant ship, who early on established his good German credentials by treating a Jewess as a member of the human race and admitting, somewhat strangely, that he wouldn't make a speech at the Führer's wedding. He also went berserk and smashed all the furniture when he learned that his splendid naval officer son had been decorated for sinking a hospital ship.

THE CHASE

Directed by Arthur Penn   1966

The Chase, an exaggerated Southern drama, in the hot-house style of William Faulkner, described what happened to a small town as it waited for the return of a young convict (Robert Redford) who had broken out of the state penitentiary and was on his way to settle old scores, not least with the lover (James Fox) of his wife (Jane Fonda).

The community was made up of a collection of unattractive and overblown caricatures. Here they all were, the destructive and the self-destructive: middle-class bigots in action, oil-rich and vulgar, drunk and lawless. It might have been *Peyton Place*. There was megalomania, wife-swapping, racism, lynching, arson and murder. 'Shoot a man for sleeping with someone's wife? That's silly,' observed one wife. 'Half the town would be wiped out.'

A chain reaction of violence ended in an orgasm of mass hysteria in a car scrapyard with petrol bombs flying, echoing the Cleveland riots at the time. The inferno was punctuated with close-ups of unconvincing extras pretending to be anonymous citizens. 'I can't stand these people,' said the sheriff, 'they're just nuts.' He was not alone. Lillian Hellman, who had adapted the story, disowned the film.

The dialogue was terrible and there was histrionic acting to match. Easily everybody's favourite character was the drunk (Martha Hyer), who knew there was a sexual revolution going on and was deeply upset that she was not part of it. She got drunker as the film progressed and was last seen eating her pearls.

Angie Dickinson and Marlon Brando in *The Chase*

Brando, as the reluctant sheriff, sick of the town, sick of his job, epitomized the spirit of *High Noon*, the only man with integrity, proud, decent, liberal, championing human rights and single-handedly risking his life to stand between the mob and total anarchy. His outspoken criticism against the violence and corruption resulted in a beating-up by three very solid citizens. The battering (very much in the *On The Waterfront* manner) was so brutal that his ability immediately afterwards to go out and do what a man had to do was frankly absurd. It was, however, his belated realization that he, too, had been bought and was owned by the town's millionaire tycoon (E.G. Marshall) which made him quit his job, as much as the bloody nose.

Marlon Brando and Robert Redford in *The Chase*

111

The sheriff, at least in Brando's introspective performance, had some depth. Invited to an orgy, he showed he had a nice way with a *double entendre.* ('With all those pistols in there, you don't need mine.') The only trouble was that he was off the screen for too long. Too much time was spent on people in whom nobody was remotely interested. There were, in fact, far too many characters without having an additional Greek chorus of two old-age pensioners as well.

Robert Redford (who spent most of the film on the run) was a good-looking convict. 'When you are willing to die,' he said, 'nobody can make you do anything any more.' His arrest and killing, as he was being taken into custody, deliberately recalled the murder of Lee Harvey Oswald by Jack Ruby. The convict, the sheriff and the sheriff's wife (Angie Dickinson) were the only likeable people in the film.

It was strange that the final image should not have been of the sheriff and his wife leaving town, reviled, rejected, yet symbolically the victors. Instead, there was a close-up of the convict's wife realizing that her husband and her lover had been killed. To lose one man in one night might have been regarded as a misfortune; to lose both in one night looked like carelessness. Jane Fonda, not surprisingly, was unequal to the facial expression required.

Angie Dickinson and
Marlon Brando in
The Chase

From the first moment we see him, Brando presents a man sunk into cavernous disillusion; a man for whom the act of finding words to communicate is already a Herculean task. There is also the familiar Brando Calvary scene wherein the actor's face is pummelled into an amorphous pudding.

Derek Prowse, *Sunday Times*

After so much cruelty and hatred, it's moving when this great actor, his face bleeding and distorted like a Kabuki mask, strides into a pool to defend the hunted convict. As in the Spiegel/Kazan *On the Waterfront*, I deplore the contrived machoism of his role, but at least his goodness is thoroughly tested – and found wanting. The atmosphere of Kazan's liberal optimism has been chilled by a new sobriety.

Eric Rhode, *New Statesman*

Brando ably plays the stereotyped champion of human rights that he seems compelled to endorse in film after film, changing only his dialect.

Time Magazine

There has always been a tendency among those who very properly loathe violence to dislike its depiction on the screen. However, it is not possible to make a film against violence without showing it; the beating-up of the sheriff is both brutal and repulsive. It is only if violence is suggested or just glimpsed that it can become titillating in this context. Luckily, in its new phase of enlightenment, the British Board of Film Censors has left it in. It would be a pity if it were attacked for this.

Ian Cameron, *Spectator*

Marlon Brando and Robert Redford in *The Chase*

113

THE APPALOOSA

Directed by Sidney J. Furie   1966
British title: *Southwest to Sonora*

The Appaloosa, a Mexican Western, was a story of revenge. A Gringo (Marlon Brando), intent on the peaceful life, rode into a Mexican border town in 1870, on a beautiful and valuable stallion (the appaloosa of the title) and headed straight for the church and confessional. He admitted to having killed a lot of men and sinned with a lot of women. The men deserved it, he said, and as for the women, well, they hadn't seemed to mind.

The movie had barely begun before the horse was stolen and Brando was being lassoed, dragged through river and bush and strung up. Single-handed, the Gringo decided to take on the whole gang, stereotyped baddies with villainously ugly faces, every one of them. 'The next time you point a gun at me, you'd better pull the trigger, because I am going to blow you into so many pieces your friends are going to get tired looking for you,' he warned their leader, played by the admirable John Saxon, who sported a big smile and an excellent set of teeth.

The two men shared a trial of strength in an elbow wrestling match in which the first hand to hit the deck would get bitten by a poisonous scorpion. The villain, unexpectedly, won. The hero lost but, perhaps, not so unexpectedly, lived to fight another day. In the end the Gringo got back not only his horse back but the bandit's girlfriend (Anjanette Comer) as well.

Initially, with his shaggy beard, straggling hair, slurred speech, filthy clothes and (according to the script) smelling like a goat, Brando looked as if he might have stepped out of a photograph of the Old West. Once he had shaved and disguised himself as a Mexican,

Marlon Brando in
The Appaloosa

115

staining his face with coffee grounds, he was his familiar brooding self, indulging in a characteristically over-long monologue in which he explained why it was so important to him to get the appaloosa back.

Sidney J. Furie constantly limited the area on the screen by blocking the view. Cameraman Russell Metty had to shoot through grills and fingers, around bottles and sombreros and over horses and cooking pots. The framing could hardly have been more

mannered and obtrusive; but it was the framing that gave *The Appaloosa* its special stamp.

The villains, in cameo roles, all gave larger-than-life, silent film performances and there were huge close-ups of their bloodshot eyes, teeth, scars and burns. As for Brando, he was accused of under-acting and certainly there was a scene early on when he didn't seem to be bothering very much, leaving all the acting to Rafael Campos.

In a role that a lesser actor might easily saunter through, Brando handicaps himself with a fiercely concentrated acting style more suitable for great occasions. He seems determined to play not just a man but a whole concept of humanity, and Saxon's brazen theft of the hoss soon looms as a cause equal in significance to the Magna Carta or the Declaration of Human Rights.

Time Magazine

Although Marlon Brando is both the star and central figure in *The Appaloosa*, he somehow contrives to give the impression that he is also giving a guest performance – or, more accurately, two guest performances – in somebody else's picture.

Arthur Knight, *Saturday Review*

Brando falls back on his old tricks of slow timing, broken lines and self-conscious mumbling.

Richard L. Coe, *Washington Post*

Mr Brando gives his usual self-indulgent display, complete with a repertory of mannerisms; yet it is, also as usual, a magnetic performance, though becoming less so inevitably, with familiarity.

Patrick Gibbs, *Daily Telegraph*

Marlon Brando in
The Appaloosa

A COUNTESS FROM HONG KONG

Directed by Charles Chaplin   1967

A Countess from Hong Kong was based on an idea that Chaplin had been carrying around since 1931 and which, originally, he had intended to make as a vehicle for his then wife, Paulette Goddard, and Gary Cooper. The movie felt like a typical 1930s Hollywood comedy and it would have been far better to have played it as a period piece, rather than to pretend it was happening in the sixties.

A Countess from Hong Kong was set in the state rooms of a luxury ocean liner and described the romance between the Ambassador-elect to Saudi Arabia and a stowaway, a former White Russian emigrée, now a penniless *poule de luxe*, making a bid to escape from a life of dance hall and prostitution.

The script, a familiar Chaplinesque mix of farce and sentimentality, was unashamedly romantic. The direction was dull and unimaginative. The camerawork was flat. The colour was second-rate. The jokes were coarse. There were jokes about belching, going to the lavatory and large bras. There were jokes about being seasick. (The ship, oddly, remained remarkably steady, even during the roughest weather.) There were jokes about girls wearing men's pyjamas and chaps sleeping on sofas. All the wellworn clichés of the 'screwball' comedies were revived.

What the movie needed, however, was some genuine 1930s sophistication: the polish, wit, innuendo and visual storytelling Ernst Lubitsch had brought to *Trouble in Paradise*, for instance. *A Countess from Hong Kong* would certainly have benefited from the stylish playing of Herbert Marshall and Kay

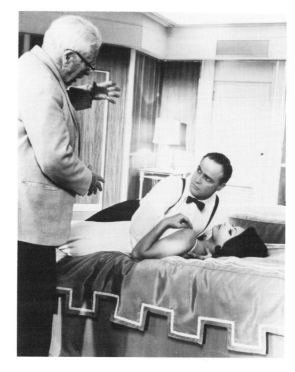

Charles Chaplin directing Marlon Brando and Sophia Loren in *A Countess from Hong Kong*

Francis in that particular film.

Brando, an unlikely choice, looked ill at ease as the Ambassador-elect, who found himself compromised. Sadly, the possibility of a scandal never existed, even in farcical terms, because the Ambassador himself never once took the possibility of scandal seriously. Brando, given no character to play and no witty lines, decided to play the role totally straight. There was one amusing moment when he was chasing Sophia Loren round the sofa. 'Take off those pyjamas or I'll tear them off! You heard me! Take them off!!' But if there was any sex going on, it all took place off-screen. There was also some well-timed farce when Brando and Loren leapt out

119

of their skins every time the doorbell rang, scuttling for cupboard and bathroom, but the gag wore thin, repeated too often.

Loren, in a beautiful dress, which managed to be both backless and frontless, was encouraged to mug. You could see Chaplin in her performance. You could also see Chaplin in Patrick Cargill's silent comedy routine of going to bed, an incongruous interlude, which would have been funnier at half the length and without cutaway shots of Loren looking amazed (a feat she found difficult to register convincingly) and which were superfluous anyway. Cargill was cast as the ambassador's valet.

There was a characteristic cameo by a bedridden and bewildered Margaret Rutherford, while Chaplin himself appeared twice in the movie, peering round the door as an elderly, seasick steward.

The Countess from Hong Kong is probably the best movie ever made by a 77-year-old man. Unhappily, it is the worst ever made by Charlie Chaplin.

Time Magazine

The romance, the heart of the story, is handled by Brando and Loren with about as much passion as that of a pair of love-wracked halibuts.

Hollis Alpert, *Saturday Review*

Marlon Brando, whose attempt to portray a wealthy US diplomat proves once again he knows *nothing* about acting.

Elaine Rothschild, *Films in Review*

In many of his films, Brando seems to move at a gentler pace, to exist on a more introspective plane, than the actors around him. His approach to drama is complex and ambiguous, based on a private paradox. He indulges in an extravagantly mannered technique, yet his performances come over as almost shockingly natural: it is the *other* people on the screen who are exposed as 'actors'. Expressing a wildly romantic temperament in ultra-realistic terms, his acting is slow, masochistic, subjective and sophisticated.

Francis Wyndham, *Sunday Times*

John Paul, Sydney Chaplin, Patrick Cargill, Marlon Brando and Sophia Loren in *A Countess from Hong Kong*

Sophia Loren and Marlon Brando in *A Countess from Hong Kong*

121

REFLECTIONS IN A GOLDEN EYE

Directed by John Huston   1967

I'm of the opinion that Brando is one of the finest actors alive. He reaches down to some recess at the end of some cavern in his spirit and comes up with a revelation of something that's new and unexpected and shocking.

John Huston quoted by Gerald Pratley
The Cinema of John Huston

Carson McCullers' bizarre and atmospheric Southern drama was a story of infidelity, militarization, perversion and murder, set in a US camp in Georgia. The novella had had an unfavourable reception in 1941, many critics finding the hothouse lusts and jealousies too grotesque to be palatable. It was hardly surprising then when the film received a 'Condemned' certificate rating from the National Catholic Office for Motion Pictures.

Major Weldon Penderton (Marlon Brando) had a sad penchant for becoming enamoured of his wife's lovers; yet despite his erotic obsessions, he lived a most rigid and unemotional life, going no further than a collection of photographs of Greek statues, which were there not so much for the major's personal satisfaction as for the audience's unsubtle enlightenment, just in case they might have missed that he was a latent homosexual.

Penderton, keenly sensitive to luxury, was a finicky dresser. He pulled weights, applied rejuvenating cream (to little visible effect) and spent much of his time in front of the mirror, making pathetic attempts to rehearse himself into gaiety or stoicism: scowling, smiling, even saluting his reflection.

Marlon Brando in
*Reflections in a
Golden Eye*

122

Marlon Brando and
Elizabeth Taylor in
*Reflections in a
Golden Eye*

He cut a comic figure on horseback, sitting rigid as a ramrod in the saddle. He was constantly humiliated by the superb horsewomanship of his wife, Leonara, who compared him unfavourably to her horse. 'Firebird is a stallion,' she taunted him. There was an exciting sequence when the horse bolted and he beat it savagely until he lost consciousness. When she learned what her husband had done to Firebird, she whipped him in front of her guests.

It was said that Leonara feared neither man nor beast nor devil. A flamboyantly vulgar Elizabeth Taylor was very funny. 'Have you ever been dragged out into the streets and thrashed by a naked woman?' she asked. At

one point she stripped naked. 'You disgust me,' said Penderton. There was an unforgettable close-up of Brando, taken from the bottom of the stairs, when Penderton threatened to kill her.

Weak and indecisive, vulnerable and isolated, the major yearned for the camaraderie of the barracks, absurdly idealizing the life of the men in the ranks. 'They're never lonely and I sometimes envy them.' He was, in fact, in love with the loneliest of lonely young soldiers, a moronic voyeur (Robert Forster), who had a penchant for riding naked through the woods and squatting silently by Leonara's bed, content to observe her from the shadows. There was a very amusing shot of the prissy major's absolutely livid face when he caught the soldier riding bare-arsed.

Brando had a good scene when he broke down during a lecture on leadership. There was, too, an extraordinary, degrading moment, very embarrassing to watch, when having thrashed the horse, his whole face crumbled into tears like a child's.

The story ended in comi-tragedy when the major, thinking the soldier was coming to see him, quickly combed his hair, only to find the boy slipping into his wife's room. He shot him dead, the swinging camera complementing Leonara's hysterics.

Julie Harris played a mad next-door neighbour, wife to Leonara's lover, who had cut off her nipples with a pair of garden shears. 'You call that normal!' shrieked Leonara. 'GARDEN SHEARS!'

Marlon Brando has been miscast as the problem husband. With his nervous twitching and self-interruptions he impresses one less as a man in the grip of a sex obsession than he does as an actor who is in doubt as what to do next.

Thomas Quinn Curtiss, *Herald Tribune*

Marlon Brando's performance as the major starts with a curiously pinched look around the nostrils and an accent so coagulated that the dialogue seems about to be slaughtered at birth. Not affectation, though it sounds like it, but the actor's way in to a characterisation of secretive pressures and unnerving, muffled smiles.

Penelope Houston, *Spectator*

John Huston and Marlon Brando on the set of *Reflections in a Golden Eye*

But somewhere the interest – Brando's not ours – flags; though even at half-voltage he's the actor you always watch. One hopes his temporary retirement from acting won't harden into a permanency.

Margaret Hinxman, *Sunday Telegraph*

The film boasts one of Marlon Brando's most wilfully perverse performances.

John Russell Taylor, *The Times*

Brando's Captain Penderton is a riveting portrait of a man sick with impossible love and sickened by it.

Paul Mayersberg, *New Society*

CANDY

Directed by Christian Marquand   1968

Candy, freely adapted from the bestselling pornographic spoof by Terry Southern and Mason Hoffenberg, was a loud-mouthed, long-winded, all-star cock-up.

Candy was a nubile dumb blonde, a luscious innocent, a sort of twentieth-century female Candide, who believed love made the world go round. Sex took place in cars, moving trucks, planes, police cars, men's rooms, hospitals, Oriental temples and also on pool tables and grand pianos. Candy was played by the Swedish actress, Ewa Aulin.

The cast included: Richard Burton as a long-haired, vain and debauched Welsh poet; Ringo Starr as a Mexican gardener; Charles Coburn as a fashionable surgeon who performed in front of an audience ('No admission after the first incision'); Walter Matthau as a mad militarist; and Charles Aznavour as a maniacal hunchback.

Brando's role was a phoney Guru, who was more interested in the pleasures of the flesh than those of the spirit. He had long, lank hair, a caste mark on his forehead, a sitar-twanging accent and a private temple in the back of his pantechnicon. His scene was an acrobatic satire of the *Kama Sutra*, the joke being that when he came to teach Candy the seven stages of sexual mysticism, he was exhausted long before he reached the seventh stage.

For all its visual daring it somehow makes sex seem childishly innocent, and at times downright tedious.

Cecil Wilson, *Daily Mail*

Marlon Brando and Ewa Aulin in *Candy*

It's all so broad on such an abysmally low and tasteless level that one wonders not so much why it was made, but how it managed to emerge from relatively respectable sources. And in fact, it's not the sex or the leering equivalent of it furnished by Candy, that in any way disturbs. It's those mentalities behind it.

Hollis Alpert, *Saturday Review*

In its contempt for its audience, the film cannot be bothered with such niceties as acting.

Time Magazine

Marlon Brando in *Candy*

THE NIGHT OF THE FOLLOWING DAY

Directed by Hubert Cornfield   1969

A teenage heiress was kidnapped at Orly airport by a man dressed as her father's chauffeur and taken to a deserted seaside villa on the Normandy coast. The hazy landscape with its dunes, wide beaches and solitary lighthouse provided the perfect hallucinatory setting for an existential French thriller, much of it shot in silence.

The chauffeur (Marlon Brando) was the leader of a gang which included a sadistic psychopath (Richard Boone), a drug addict (Rita Moreno), who sniffed cocaine in rolled dollar bills, and a lumbering moron (Jess Hahn). The gang, as is the way in this sort of movie, fell out and killed each other before they could enjoy the ransom money.

Marlon Brando,
Richard Boone,
Pamela Franklin in
*The Night of the
Following Day*

Marlon Brando,
Rita Moreno and
Jess Hahn in
*The Night of the
Following Day*

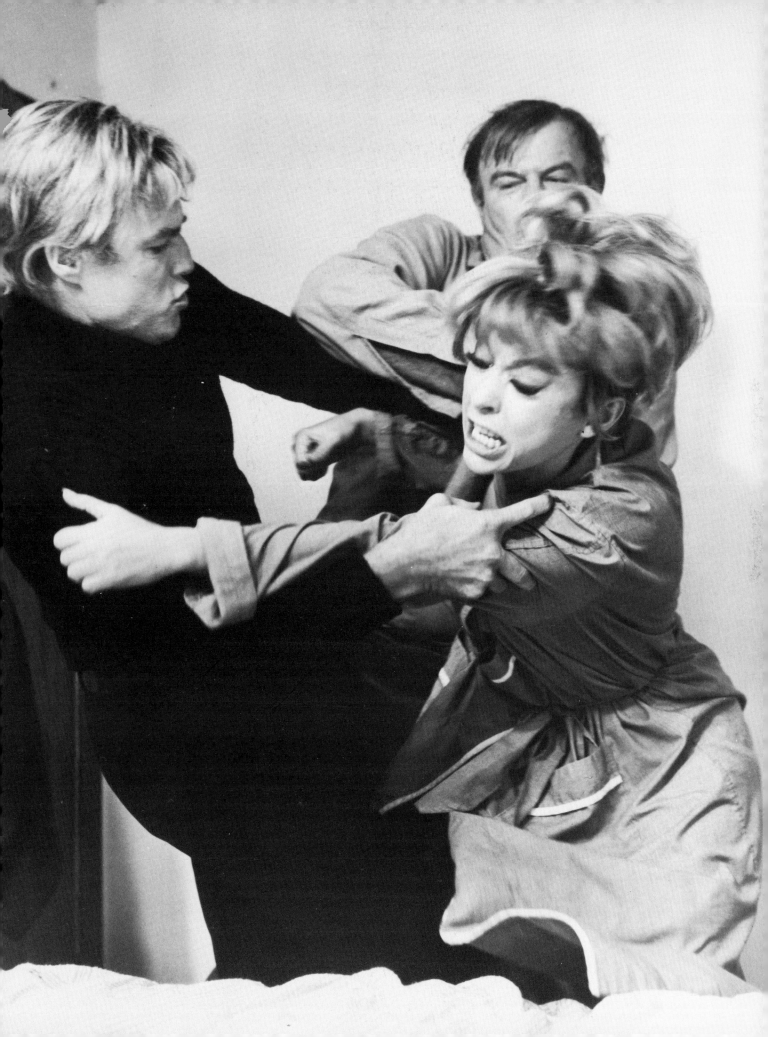

The heiress (Pamela Franklin) was highly emotional. Her brother said she was always dreaming things up, so much so that her family never knew whether she was speaking the truth or not. In this particular instance, in a not too unexpected denouement, the events described turned out to have been figments of her imagination, a dream turned nightmare, ending with her strung up. (The violence was edited out in some versions.) At the end of the film the girl was still on the plane. But as she came out of Orly airport, she was met by the same chauffeur, smiling in an equivocal way, his greeting drowned by the roar of an overhead aircraft.

Brando, in a blond wig, was dressed all in black – black trousers, black jumper, black belt, black gloves – and he looked both astonishingly young and astonishingly slim. He was much the nicest member of the gang. There were admittedly times when it did seem as if he was sending himself up, especially when he was saying things like, 'There aren't going to be any more rainbows, man,' or smashing a bottle and holding it to Rita Moreno's face. 'I love you. Go on, cut my face if that's what you feel like – I deserve it.'

There were indeed moments when it seemed as if the film was also sending up Brando, especially when the girl's brother, listening to a tape, identified the kidnapper's voice with a remark to the effect that he had a way of slurring his words. It was a private joke, which the public could enjoy.

There was a memorable shot of Brando, rising from the sea, having just killed the Boone character. It was a shot which would be recalled later, when Martin Sheen rose from the murky waters, knife in mouth, to kill Brando, in his role of Kurtz, in *Apocalypse Now*.

Once again in a film good enough to match his talents, he demonstrates conclusively in *Night* that his powers remain undiminished by intervening years of sloppiness and self-indulgence. It is good to have him back.

Time Magazine

It is lamentable that Brando who might be in something by Buñuel or Losey or Pasolini, has wasted his time in such commonplace stuff.

Thomas Quinn Curtiss, *Herald Tribune*

As far as acting is concerned, he walks through all the nonsense with a kind of dazed disdain, occasionally amusing himself by giving an excellent imitation of Brando.

Penelope Houston, *Observer*

It may seem unfair to attempt to judge his – or anyone's – acting in such a silly film as this, but it is nevertheless true that in the past Brando, by his sheer presence and talent, was able to make of his performance something worth experiencing, regardless of the merits of the film. This is no longer true. It would be interesting to know why. Were the seeds of his decline already present in the earlier work? Was he, to change the cliché, just a shooting star? Or more depressingly, would we, if we could see his earlier work again, decide he never was that good anyhow? Or, most hopefully, is he only in that kind of early middle-age cocoon which often precedes the full flowering of maturity?

Richard Roud, *Guardian*

Rita Moreno and Marlon Brando in *The Night of the Following Day*

The 1970s

QUEIMADA!

Directed by Gillo Pontecorvo   1970
English title: *Burn!*

Civilisation belongs to the whites. What sort
of civilisation? And until when?

Sir William Walter

Queimada! described the making and
breaking of a peasant revolutionary, José
Dolores. The setting was the fictional island of
Queimada, a Portuguese sugar colony in the
Caribbean in the mid-nineteenth century. The
film had originally been called *Quemada*
until the Spanish government said they would
ban the picture, not wishing to be reminded of
an inglorious episode in their colonial history.
Quemada was the name Spain had given to
an island they had deliberately burnt in the
sixteenth century. The producers then
changed the title to the Portuguese spelling,
because the Portuguese box-office receipts
were less important to the American
distributors. 'Queimada' means 'burnt' in
Portuguese.

The British government, wanting to end the
Portuguese monopoly in the sugar trade, sent
an *agent provocateur* to the island of
Queimada to stir up a rebellion among the
ruthlessly exploited slaves. The uprising was a
great success and the Portuguese were kicked
out. The island got its independence and a
puppet government, beholden to British
interests, was put in its place.

Ten years later a British sugar company
invited the agent back as a military advisor to
help them crush another slave uprising and,
in particular, the revolutionary leader he
had so successfully created. But in order to
destroy Dolores, the agent also had to destroy

Marlon Brando
in *Queimada!*

134

the very sugar plantations on which the
island's prosperity depended.

Brando was cast as the agent, Sir William
Walker, an immeasurably civilised adventurer
with a nice line in cynical wit. It was never
quite clear whose interest Sir William was
serving; but then he himself wasn't certain
why he was doing what he was doing, apart,
that was, from the money. Perhaps, he said,
he had nothing else to do. Always a political

realist, he dealt and played his cards with
enigmatic and ruthless detachment, claiming
he was not the author of the atrocities he
committed, but only the instrument, an
argument which failed to impress his black
protégé, who spat in his face. Dolores,
morally Sir William's superior, refused to
take an opportunity to escape, preferring to
be hanged and give his people the martyr the
revolution needed for it to carry on.

136

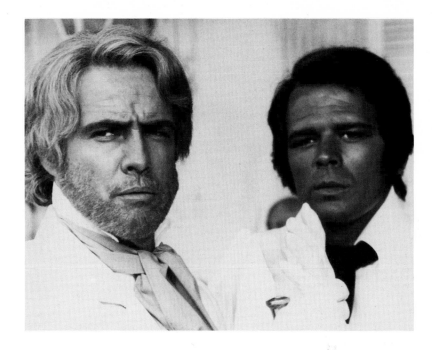

The great strength of Brando's performance was the way he was able to suggest,
with insufficient help from the script, that
underneath the smooth and insidious
sang-froid there was a guilty idealist, who
despised himself as much as he did his
paymasters.

Brando, rueful and cool, always equal to the
complexities and ambiguities of the role,
acted with notable intelligence. The upper-
class English accent, far less affected than
the one he had used in *Mutiny on the Bounty*,
was impeccable. His murder by the quayside
by a dark porter was a tremendous shock.

Evaristo Marquez, an illiterate Colombian
cane-cutter, who spoke only his native tongue
and had never seen a movie, let alone acted in
one, was cast as Dolores, a man made
vulnerable only by his lack of education.
Marquez, powerful in physique, presented a
striking and dignified presence. Inevitably, as
an actor, he was not in the same league as
Brando; but having said that, his
performance, judged by any standard and
however achieved, was truly astonishing.

Quiemada! began with arresting, burning
credit titles. The film was not always easy to
follow. The action was confusing, the dialogue
was stilted, the dubbing was clumsy and the
editing was ruthless. Nevertheless, the film
had an epic, majestic sweep and the set pieces
– such as the carnival ending in the
assassination of the president, the flushing
out of the guerrillas by burning the sugar
cane, the coldblooded massacres and the
soldiers advancing through a burnt landscape
littered with corpses – all these scenes
showed tremendous cinematic flair. The
images were beautiful, brutal and unforgettable. The photography was by Marcello Gatti.

There was a good performance by Renato
Salvatori as the well-meaning, moderate
president and there was also a superb score
by Ennio Morricone.

Marlon Brando and
Renato Salvatori
in *Quemada!*

**Brando may have problems but type-casting is not
one of them. He is never the same man twice. This
actor's passion for false accents is equalled only
by Olivier's passion for false noses.**

Cecil Wilson, *Daily Mail*

**He gives, as ever, a remarkable performance. But
it is a very Brandoish creation, undershot with
psychological tensions which the story itself
doesn't support. It becomes a burden on the film,
deflecting it from its proper use.**

Nora Hibbin, *Morning Star*

**A certain narcissistic element keeps intruding, but
at its best Brando is good enough to remind us
what a good actor he can be when he lets himself.**

John Russell Taylor, *The Times*

Overleaf:
Marlon Brando and
Evaristo Marquez in
Queimada!

137

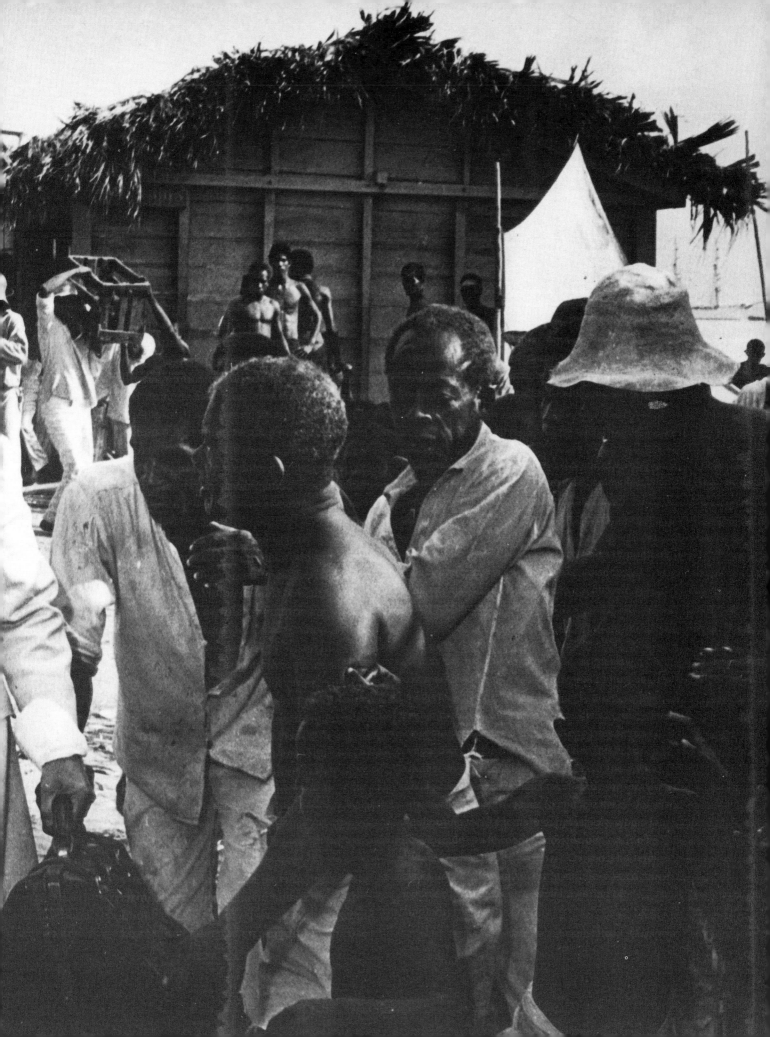

THE NIGHTCOMERS

Directed by Michael Winner 1971

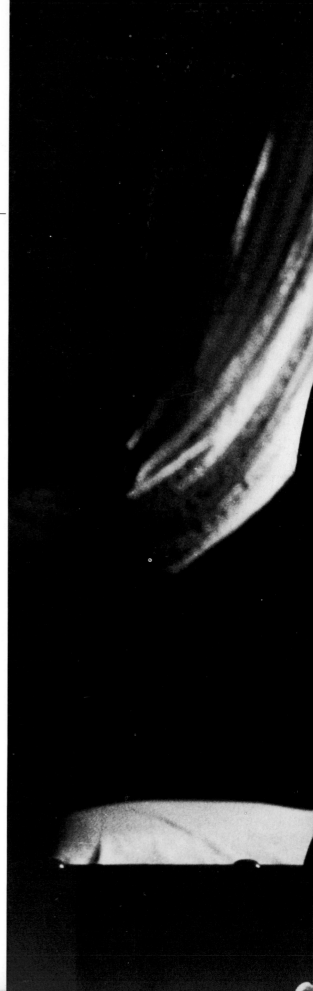

I think it is a most wonderful, lurid, poisonous little tale, like an Elizabethan tragedy. I am greatly impressed by it. James is developing, but he will never arrive at passion, I fear.

Oscar Wilde in a letter to Robert Ross, 1899

Henry James had the story of *The Turn of the Screw* from Edward Benson, Archbishop of Canterbury, who, in his turn, had had it from his sister. This classic novella, a macabre mystery of uncanny ugliness, horror and pain, built up a sense of evil without ever stating what the evil was.

Michael Winner's prequel, characteristically making precise what James deliberately had left ambiguous, actually showed Peter Quint and Miss Jessel, the valet and governess, indulging in sado-masochism which the young children, Miles and Flora, later re-enacted with amusing results. The youngsters' corruption was mere horseplay.

The Nightcomers both over-simplified and sensationalized the original story, introducing such unnecessary Gothic horrors as pins in wax dolls, dolls buried in chamber-pots, and worst of all, exploding frogs. The enigma of James was infinitely preferable to the explicitness of Winner for, as James well knew, the moment 'the veil is lifted, all mystery disappears, and with it all sense of terror'. There was more terror in the elegant, black and white version, *The Innocents*, directed by Jack Clayton ten years earlier, in which Deborah Kerr had played the governess.

In the novella, Peter Quint was a good-

Marlon Brando and Stephanie Beacham in *The Nightcomers*

looking, impudent valet, who had close, red, curly hair. In the film, he was a surly, burly, loutish gardener with straggling, shoulder-length hair. In the novella, Quint was described as base, menial, spoiled, depraved. The fellow was a hound. He did what he wished. He was so clever and so deep. Mrs Gosse, the housekeeper, thought he must have been an actor.

In the film, Marlon Brando was not so much James's agent of evil as an Irish rogue, a compulsive and hypnotic storyteller, who was able to dominate the children by his macabre tales. Thus, the children, who saw the world almost entirely through Quint's eyes, came to believe that everything he told them was true and so when he said that if you really loved somebody you wanted to kill them, they genuinely thought he and their governess would be much happier dead and decided to help them on their way. Miles shot Quint with his bow and arrow and a boat was sabotaged so that Miss Jessel drowned.

Jessel was a willing partner in Quint's sado-masochistic games. Stephanie Beacham conveyed perfectly the absurdity of her mixture of outward Victorian prudery and inner lust. When Jessel pretended it was such a shame that their relationship had to end in bondage and whipping, Quint told her she was talking a lot of 'bullshit'. When she then started to imply that had she known from the beginning what it was going to be like, he interrupted her with 'more bullshit'. In the same sequence when she had the temerity to suggest that Quint lived in a pigsty, he reacted in a way which Stanley Kowalski would immediately have recognized and

approved. 'I'LL GIVE YOU PIGSTY!' he yelled, sloshing her about.

The screenplay did not attempt to emulate James's elegance and fastidiousness. 'You're scum!' shrieked Mrs Gosse. 'Your wrinkled arse!' retorted Quint. Thora Hird was not Henry James's simple, wholesome house-keeper and emerged by far the most unpleasant character in the film.

Brando was charming with the children and there was an excellent scene when he was telling them how his father had tried to sell a hack as a thoroughbred. The story, which began amusingly enough, ended with a great bellow of pain, bringing back, as it did, memories of his own cruel upbringing.

There are times when this extraordinary actor, as Quint, seems to be in another film entirely, looking like a slightly mad Ben Franklin, and then there are small, beautiful moments when Brando's intelligence creates a truly complex character.

Vincent Canby, *New York Times*

There is always a sense of something unpredictable and dangerous – perhaps most of all a talent more often misused than used but still worryingly, excitingly there.

John Russell Taylor, *The Times*

Brando, 20 years on from Stanley Kowalski, still has the presence to make bullying cruelty captivating.

Timothy Foote, *Time Magazine*

Stephanie Beacham
and Marlon Brando
in *The Nightcomers*

THE GODFATHER

Directed by Francis Ford Coppola 1972

> There's nothing personal in this. It's business.
> . . . We're not murderers despite what the
> undertakers say.
>
> Don Vito Corleone

The Godfather was *the* gangster movie of the
1970s and its real subject matter was a
demonstration of how the American Mafia
organization works. Here was crime as big
business with board meetings. 'I always
wanted,' said Francis Ford Coppola, 'to use
the Mafia as a metaphor for America.'

Many people felt that the movie not only
humanized the Mafia, but that it also glorified
and romanticized their power, wealth,
brutality, corruption and political influence.
So ambiguous was the film's attitude that it
was widely believed to have been made with
their approval. It was reported that some of
them had appeared as extras in the wedding
sequence.

Brando was cast as Don Vito Corleone, the
head of one of the five Mafia families; though
out of deference to the Italian-American Civil
Rights League (who didn't like Italians being
portrayed as gangsters and gangsters being
portrayed as Italians) words like Mafia and
Cosa Nostra were never used.

Everybody was on the Don's payroll:
politicians, judges, cops, newspapermen. The
actual first sight of Brando was a shock. The
face was crusty, craggy, all dried-up; the
complexion was sallow; the temples and
moustache were grey; the skin was pock-
marked; the cheeks were puffed out (he wore
an elaborate mouth plate to make his jowls

Salvatori Corsitto
and Marlon Brando
in *The Godfather*

144

heavy); the voice was husky, rasping yet strangely quiet; the eyes were sad, weary, dead. He looked so old and as the film progressed he got even older. In real life Brando was only 47. Up there on the screen he was well into his seventies.

Very early on, there was a shot of him with his back to the camera, head leaning on his hand in a listening position, which recalled the single shot of the Mafia boss in *On the Waterfront*. Later, there was a marvellous shot of his grief-stricken face when he learned of his eldest son's death. It was a powerful face, a face to be put up on Mount Rushmore, alongside Washington, Jefferson, Roosevelt and Lincoln.

Brando, portly, paternal, deceptively gentle, tempered Corleone with a listless shrug and a flick of the hand. His sentimental

Abe Vigoda,
Marlon Brando,
John Cazale,
Al Lettieri and
Robert Duvall in
The Godfather

Victor Redina,
Richard Conte and
Marlon Brando in
The Godfather

death scene, as he played with his grandson in the garden, was as unexpected as it was moving and given an added irony and poignancy when the little boy pretended to gun him down with a hand pesticide spray. The scene looked as if it was being improvised, especially when Corleone stuffed his mouth full of orange peel to amuse him and the boy, suddenly frightened by the monster-face, burst into tears.

The set pieces – the long wedding sequence which opened the film, the nailing and garrotting of a hit man, the murder on the highway, the murder in the restaurant, the gunning of Corleone himself in the street, the strangulation in the car – all these were brilliantly handled by Francis Ford Coppola.

The Godfather ended memorably with two baptisms, two rituals: one sacred, the other profane. At the very moment that Al Pacino (in his role of the Don's favourite son) was renouncing Satan and all his works in the Cathedral at the baptism of his son, so were his henchmen massacring his rivals all over the city. The constant cross-cutting from font to blood-bath was electrifying.

The special strength of Pacino's beautifully controlled and eminently plausible transition from innocence to ruthlessness was that when he finally became the Godfather, Marlon Brando's presence was unmistakably there in his performance.

In this part, Marlon Brando gives the greatest performance of a great career.

Felix Barker, *Evening News*

There is no longer any need to talk tragically of Marlon Brando's career. His stormy two-decade odyssey through films good and bad, but rarely big enough to house his prodigious talents, has ended in triumph . . . At forty-seven, the king has returned to claim his throne.

Newsweek

Brando's triumph and fascination is less that of an actor of parts than of a star galaxy of myths. Which is to say that he does not so much lose himself in his part as lift his part to his own exalted level as a star personality.

Andrew Sarris, *Village Voice*

Curious casting, but deeply satisfying in a studied, actorish way. For Mr Brando is a master of timing. He holds us almost literally in the palm of his hand as he uses it to search for a word. It is easy to believe in his domestic authority.

Eric Shorter, *Daily Telegraph*

Despite clever make-up and the best imitation of Humphrey Bogart's voice I have yet heard, Brando is on to a loser here. So are most of the other actors whose performances range from the competent to the quite nakedly ham.

Phil Cohen, *Morning Star*

Al Pacino and
Marlon Brando in
The Godfather

L'ULTIMO TANGO A PARIGI

Directed by Bernardo Bertolucci   1972
English title: *Last Tango in Paris*

I can confirm that neither the performers nor
myself ever contemplated for a moment
commercial benefits or entertainment
devices. We were interested in the question
of possession of a relationship, a self-
destructive one prevalent in today's society.

Bernardo Bertolucci

Last Tango in Paris was so explicit in its
sexual relationship, so free with its four-letter
words, so blasphemous, so crude in its
vigorously simulated copulation, sodomy and
masturbation, so frank verbally and visually,
that it divided public and critics alike, giving
ballroom dancing a bad name and even
making the purchase of butter fraught with
embarrassment.

Paul (Marlon Brando), a middle-aged,
45-year-old American expatriate, was
walking down a street in Paris. His general
appearance was unkempt and ravaged; he
might have been mistaken for a tramp. He let
out a long drawn-out scream, worthy of
Francis Bacon (whose work figured in the
credit titles) and which could just be heard
under the roar of the traffic.

The film began as it meant to go on. There
was a brutal encounter in an empty flat with a
20-year-old French girl, Jeanne (Maria
Schneider), doll-faced, mini-skirted and
provocative. Paul ripped off her tights and,
not pausing to take off his camel hair coat,
they screwed standing up. He insisted there
should be no names, no personal relations, no
past, no future. 'I don't have a name. I don't
want to know your name. I want to know

Maria Schneider and
Marlon Brando in
Last Tango in Paris

153

nothing, nothing, nothing. We don't need names here . . . I don't want a name. Better off with a grunt or a groan for a name.'

They continued to meet in the empty flat. The traumatic experience of his wife's infidelities and inexplicable suicide had led Paul, tormented by guilt and self-loathing, to seek a kind of exorcism through sado-masochism. He constantly humiliated her, insisting on total submission to his sexual needs. There seemed nothing the girl would not do. Women's organizations objected that cinemagoers were allowed to see Schneider's pubic hair but that whenever Brando made love, it was always with his trousers on. There was, however, one moment when he did take his trousers down, disrupting a tango contest and showing his backside to an outraged female judge.

Jeanne was engaged to a young TV director (Jean-Pierre Léaud) who was making a film, *A Portrait of a Girl*, in which she starred. 'You make me do things I never do,' she grumbled. But then what he asked her to do must have seemed rather tame after requests to screw on the mantelpiece and the radiator.

There were moments of tenderness and humour, when Paul was washing her body and trying to come without touching. 'Are you concentrating?' he asked. But such moments were rare. For the most part he was brutish, needing to debase himself as much as her.

The film ended with him chasing Jeanne through the streets and up the stairs to her parents' flat. 'I love you. I want to know your name.' She shot him. Before dying, and looking very cute and charming in her father's peak cap, Brando carefully (and very

theatrically) parked his chewing gum under the balcony rail. 'I don't know who he is,' complained the bewildered girl. 'I don't know his name. He is a madman.'

Last Tango in Paris seemed, at times, to be about Brando's own life and career. There was a long monologue when he remembered his childhood and being all dressed up to go to the basketball and getting shit on his shoes and the car smelling. There was an equally long and rambling confession over the body of his dead wife (clearly improvised) when he was cursing and crying in close-up. The scene was so self-lacerating and so self-indulgent that it seemed to many that Bertolucci was exploiting Brando the man rather than Brando the actor.

Brando himself was quoted as saying that he never wanted to make another film like *Tango* ever again. 'For the first time,' he said, 'I have felt the violation of my innermost self.'

If the film achieves tragic dimensions it is because he supplies them. If the film is also funny, it is because he makes it so. When he's off-screen, there's nothing much left except style in a vacuum, in spite of Miss Schneider's fresh and unforced playing. Some actors can be brilliant without giving anything much of themselves. Brando is nothing without giving a lot. His is not a fascinating display of technique. It's a carefully ordered stripshow which isn't paralleled incidentally by the physical junketings.

Derek Malcolm, *Guardian*

Maria Schneider and Marlon Brando in *Last Tango in Paris*

Marlon Brando and
Maria Schneider in
Last Tango in Paris

Marlon Brando in
Last Tango in Paris

As Paul, Brando gives a performance of shattering intensity that draws the whole film together, lifting it above the schematic intellectualized level it might have remained on with a lesser actor (or an actor giving less of himself) in the role. He transforms *Last Tango* into an emotional experience that leaves one both totally exhausted and yet eager to see it again as soon as possible.

Philip French, *Observer*

Marlon Brando cannot express failure, except in Napoleonic terms – the raging grief, the sobbing bitterness. He cannot reduce himself. His interpretation of Paul is overwrought, part of the Brando myth. Whenever Bertolucci tries to indicate a general context, to suggest the doomed relationship is symptomatic of a wider malaise, he is blocked by the sheer bulk and magnificence of Brando's idiosyncrasy

Christopher Hudson, *Spectator*

Brando's performance is an enigma – one is continually wondering whether he is playing anyone but himself. His importance to the life of the film is most evident from the fact that when he disappears from the screen our interest virtually collapses. His absence is felt as a dramatic not emotional loss. Without him up there, it is difficult to care about what happens to anyone.

Jon Landau, *Rolling Stone*

It is very beautifully performed trash. Beneath its soft edges and tough sexual romanticism you see commercialism rampant. It is even more rampant than the sex which is always carefully contained.

Clive Barnes, *The Times*

THE MISSOURI BREAKS

Directed by Arthur Penn   1976

The Missouri Breaks, set in the foothills of the Tobacco Root Mountain, Montana, in the 1880s, was an exposure of the Western myth. Arthur Penn's slow-paced film, a mixture of dreamy, nostalgic romanticism and gritty realism, began with a long and lyrical sequence in the beautiful countryside, which led up to the casual hanging of a rustler without trial.

The rustler's leader, Tom Logan, was played by Jack Nicholson, who had just won an Oscar for his unforgettable performance in *One Flew Over the Cuckoo's Nest*. Here his face was so heavily bearded that only his eyes and teeth were visible. Logan, sexy and attractive, was not evil at all; he was just a cunning and cheeky charmer, looking for a better life. The story was built round his courtship of Jane Braxton (Kathleen Lloyd), a liberated modern woman, anxious to lose her virginity. Their raunchy sexual skirmishes were acted with appealing wit.

The rustlers were infintely preferable to the so-called good people and the opening scenes were played for knockabout, larky comedy. The incompetent robbery, which brought back memories of *Butch Cassidy and the Sundance Kid*, was carried out by immature, horseplaying hooligans. 'You boys new to this?' asked the train guard.

The film shifted gear and took on more tragic tones when the God-fearing, *Tristam Shandy*-reading baron (John McLian) took the law into his own hands (law and order being the film's theme) and hired a Regulator to rid him of the cattle and horse thieves. Brando was cast as the Regulator, a professional

Marlon Brando and Jack Nicholson in *The Missouri Breaks*

159

Marlon Brando in
The Missouri Breaks

gunman called Robert E. Lee Clayton, a name to conjure with, evoking, as it did, the Confederate general, famous for his military strategy.

Clayton arrived on a seemingly riderless horse and proceeded to ham it up immediately when he attended a funeral and took ice from the coffin to soothe his toothache. Described as a lilac-smelling son of a bitch, his effeminate manners masked a brutal and ruthless killer, who carried out his task with crazy religious fervour, quarrying his victims for his own sadistic satisfaction. 'I don't care a damn what I get paid,' he said. One by one the rustlers were tracked down. The Regulator, who had a particularly nasty way with a harpoon-shaped crucifix, was something of a practical joker. He drowned the men, burnt them out and shot them while they were fornicating and even when they were in the privy.

Brando was never the same from scene to scene, wearing a variety of garbs, including buckskin jacket, coolie hat, bandanna and

162

even appearing, for no good reason, in drag, looking like Old Mother Hubbard. The only woman Clayton admitted ever having loved was his horse. The horse got a big kiss. There was a famous scene when he was in the bath, looking as voluptuous as any Rubens nude, and he deliberately turned his back on Logan, taunting him, daring him to shoot him. Logan, unable to do so (no Charlotte Corday, he), finally shot the bath instead.

Brando and Nicholson were rarely on screen together. Some critics thought Nicholson was overshadowed. Certainly he was acting in a different style from Brando: he was much more restrained, low-key and naturalistic. His sensitive, melancholy and thoughtful performance subtly expressed his inner conflict and grief for the death of his gang.

The film led you to believe that Logan would also be killed by the Regulator and so it was a surprise of the first order when he managed to murder the sleeping Regulator first. Clayton's death scene was unforgettable. 'You know what made you wake up?' asked Logan. 'Your throat's been slit.'

In the gloomy middle years of his career, he used to demonstrate his contempt for the medium by giving the smallest part of his talents. Now he has apparently decided to give too much, to parody himself. His work in *Missouri Breaks* is not so much a performance as it is a finger thrust joyously upward by an actor who has survived everything, including his own self-destructive impulses.

Richard Schickel, *Time Magazine*

This is one of the most extravagant displays of grande-damerie since Sarah Bernhardt, and the fascination of it is not to be denied.

Russell Davies, *Observer*

Marlon Brando is a tease. He pushes the eccentricities of a character to the limits of credibility. Then, just as you are thinking 'This is ridiculous,' he drops the game.

Judith Simons, *Daily Express*

He has an unerring gift for weighing the value of a character and giving it no less and no more than it deserves.

Margaret Hinxman, *Daily Mail*

Marlon Brando at 52 has the sloppy belly of a 62-year-old, the white hair of a 72-year-old, and the total lack of discipline of a precious 12-year-old.

Fergus Cashin, *Sun*

Jack Nicholson and Marlon Brando in *The Missouri Breaks*

SUPERMAN

Directed by Richard Donner   1978

Marlon Brando,
Terence Stamp,
Jack O'Halloran and
Sarah Douglas in
Superman

This is no fantasy.

El-Jor

Superman has appeared many times on radio,
television and film since the cartoonists Jerry
Siegal and Joseph Shuster created him for
Action Comic in 1938. However, in *Superman
– The Movie*, such an inordinate time was
spent on a phoney SF prologue on the Planet
Krypton that it seemed as if the red and blue
long underwear, with matching red cape,
were never going to appear.

Krypton was a dull place, mere plastic bric-
à-brac. It was a great relief to get down to
earth and into the familiar American
landscape of Andrew Wyatt and a homely
surrogate mother, who might have been
painted by Norman Rockwell.

Marlon Brando in
Superman

Brando played El-Jor, Superman's dad,
who prophesied that the planet was about to
explode and packed off his only son to earth
seconds before it was destroyed. 'He will not
be alone,' he said, bequeathing him his
strength. 'He will never be alone. He will
travel far.' Brando spoke his lines in his best
English accent but, unfortunately, without any
humour. The biblical language ('I have sent
them you, my only son') was absurd. His wife
(Susannah York) was appalled that her baby
should be going to earth: 'They are primitives
– thousands of years behind us!'

Most newspapers and magazines showed
far more interest in the enormous amount of
money it was rumoured Brando was being
paid for twelve days' work than they did in the
actual performance. El-Jor was just a boring,
heavy, white-haired, white-robed presence.
He looked like an ageing rugby coach. As for
the rest of the cast, they had nothing to do but
play supporting roles to the falling scenery.

Twenty-four-year-old Christopher Reeve,
in the title role, differentiated nicely between
Superman and Clark Kent, judging the
demarcation line between the straight and
the camp perfectly.

**As for Brando, even he is not immune from the
film's unhappy knack of reducing talent to nil.**

Nicholas Wapshott, *Scotsman*

Brando is never less than faintly ridiculous.

Andrew Weiner, *New Society*

APOCALYPSE NOW

Directed by Francis Ford Coppola   1979

The most important thing I wanted to do in the making of *Apocalypse Now* was to create a film experience that would give its audience a sense of the horror, the madness, the sensuousness and the moral dilemma of the Vietnam War.

Francis Ford Coppola

The long-awaited *Apocalypse Now* was based on Joseph Conrad's *The Heart of Darkness*, though there was no acknowledgement on the screen to Conrad's novella. The film, a powerful statement on the obscenity of war, was excitingly staged and brilliantly photographed, spectacular in its exploding colour, sound and images.

'I don't want the film to be about war,' said Coppola. 'I want it to be *the* war.' *Apocalyse Now* was the ultimate trip, with everybody freaked out, high on drugs, high on fear, hooked on the sheer beauty of horror and the orgiastic excitement of mindless arbitrary killing. In the words of the song, all the children were insane. Vietnam was the arsehole of the world. The bullshit piled so quickly you needed wings to stay above it.

The Marlow of the novel had been transformed into Captain Willard (Martin Sheen, first-rate) a burned-out intelligence officer, a former CIA killer, who was sent on a mission to find and terminate Colonel Kurtz 'with extreme prejudice' (military-speak for assassinate). His nightmarish, hallucinatory voyage down river through the jungle, was an extraordinary and unforgettable journey through Hell, a shattering psychological blow to a man already emotionally unbalanced. When Willard finally met up with Kurtz, there was no real confrontation. He was merely the passive listener. He had already seen the horror.

Colonel Walter E. Kurtz was one of the most outstanding officers the US had ever produced. A man of wit and humour, a humanitarian, he had thrown off his military responsibility, retreated into the Cambodian jungle and set up his own private army of mad Montagnard tribesmen and renegade soldiers. The army, worshipping him like a god, operated without any decent restraint, following his every order, however ridiculous it might be.

True to Conrad, Marlon Brando was, at first, little more than a voice and all that was

Marlon Brando
in *Apocalypse Now*

Kurtz's kingdom
in *Apocalypse Now*

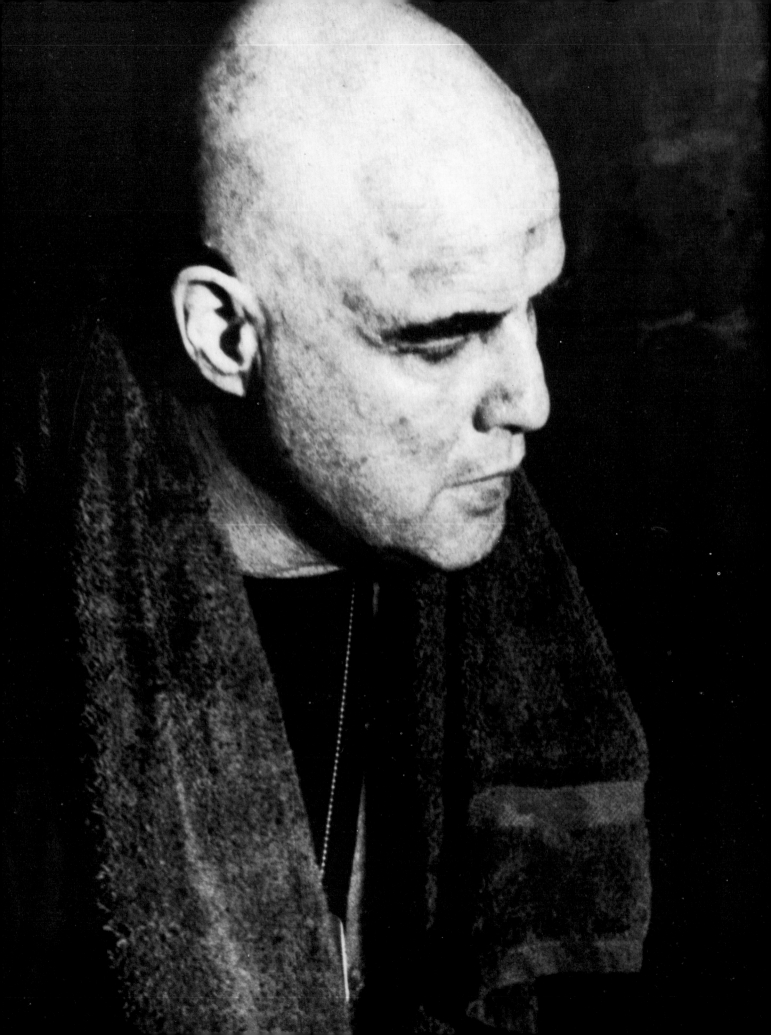

seen of him, by a flickering light, was part of the huge dome of his ivory-bald head, which he stroked and washed. His face remained in impenetrable darkness for a long time; the face, in fact, was not seen until the moment when Willard, in answer to the specific question as to whether he was an assassin, replied that he was a soldier. Kurtz corrected him: 'You're an errand boy sent by grocers' clerks to collect the dough.'

Brando's Buddha-like Kurtz, vast, hulking, grotesque, was a formidable, frightening presence: a mad Minotaur in his murky labyrinth, waiting to be killed. His intelligence concentrated upon himself with horrible intensity. Nobody wanted his death more than he did.

Brando had a long, rambling monologue (too obviously improvised) in which Kurtz tried to explain how he had come to be what he was. He remembered a time when he had been with Special Forces and he had gone into a camp and inoculated children for polio and after they had gone the Viet Cong had come and hacked off every inoculated arm.

There was one horrific moment when Kurtz personally delivered a decapitated head to Willard. Brando towered above Sheen. His face, painted with a down-turned mouth, was photographed and lit from below. He looked like some fierce warrior from an ancient Oriental drama. He was worse than crazy. He was evil.

There was a splendid performance by Robert Duvall as a death-and-glory air cavalry officer in a black stetson, who behaved as if he were in a John Ford movie. He was having such a good time ('I love the smell of napalm

This and previous pages: Marlon Brando and Martin Sheen in *Apocalypse Now*

170

in the morning. It smells of victory') that he couldn't bear the thought of the war ending. This strutting maniac, a savage indictment of military idiocy, was involved in one of the film's most memorable sequences, the helicopter raid to destroy a village just so his boys could surf on the beach. The raid, brilliantly staged and edited, accompanied by Wagner's *The Ride of Valkyries* blaring from the helicopters' speakers, was as exhilarating as it was terrible.

King Kong would have recognized Kurtz's kingdom in the jungle, with its crumbling temples, sculptures and sacrificial altars. It was a wonderful setting for pagan idolatry and unspeakable rites. The dressing, with its naked, painted warriors, hanging corpses, decapitated heads, rotting bodies and skulls, was highly theatrical. 'Sometimes he goes too far; he is the first to admit it,' observed a photo-journalist (Dennis Hopper), a crazy, raving hippie, completely in awe of Kurtz and talking garbage. The set, based on Angkor Wat, was an unforgettable image of Kurtz's power and corruption.

Though there were no acknowledgements to Conrad, there were acknowledgements to John Weston's *From Ritual to Romance* and Sir James Fraser's *The Golden Bough*, both of which just happened to be lying around Kurtz's pied-à-terre, while Kurtz himself quoted from T.S. Eliot's *The Hollow Men*. Vietnam was The Waste Land.

Coppola (who made an ironic appearance as a TV director yelling at the soldiers to ignore the camera) admitted he had no idea how to end the film. There were many people who thought the proposed ditched ending of

the assault and destruction of Kurtz's kingdom should have been kept in.

The horror of filming on location in the Philippines, the enormous financial and logistical difficulties, the earthquakes and typhoons, plus Martin Sheen's heart attack, have all been recorded in a fascinating documentary by Coppola's wife.

Only Brando could have held up the broken back of Coppola's film at this crucial juncture. He does it by force of personality and performance. As unpredictable as ever, he has you hanging on his words, sluggishly dragged out of himself, but so idiosyncratically spoken that the total effect is a triumph of the unpredictable approach over the all-too-predictable philosophizing.

Alexander Walker, *Evening Standard*

It succeeds brilliantly up to the last reel, when Brando himself enters. Then, astonishingly, all credibility and authenticity evaporates as symbolism and fantasy take over.

John du Pre, *Sunday People*

Only when Brando, shaven-headed, bloated and Buddha-like, makes his appearance in the last quarter of the film does the suspense relax. Brando has been over-rated for years. He is a piece of ham in a film that is raw meat.

Arthur Thirkell, *Daily Mirror*

ROOTS: THE NEXT GENERATIONS

Directed for television by John Erman, Charles S. Dubin,
George Stanford Brown and Lloyd Richards   1979

The second series of Alex Hayley's
enormously popular *Roots* traced Hayley's
ancestors from 1882 to 1967.

Marlon Brando appeared in episode 7, cast
as George Lincoln Rockwell, the leader of the
American Nazi Party. His performance won
an Emmy.

Marlon Brando in
*Roots: The Next
Generations*

The 1980s/ 1990s

Marlon Brando in
The Formula

THE FORMULA

Directed by John G. Avildsen   1980

Money, not morality, is the principle commerce of civilized nations.

Thomas Jefferson

The Formula was an incomprehensible and exceedingly convoluted political thriller about oil tycoons and multinational cartels willing to do anything, even murder, to suppress a formula for converting coal into cheap synthetic oil so that they could cash in on the oil shortage. The actual facts on which author Steve Shagan had based his fiction were infinitely more interesting than the plodding claptrap on offer. There was far too much talk and not nearly enough suspense. Anti-climax followed anti-climax.

Brando played the all-powerful head of one such cartel, a self-satisfied and cynical hoodlum, living in an ivory tower. His head was partly shaved. He wore rimless spectacles and false upper teeth with a specially wide upper plate. He also wore a hearing-aid (so that his lines could be fed to him by radio, it was said). He resembled a gigantic bullfrog and looked as if he had stepped not only into one of Sydney Greenstreet's old roles but also into one of his old suits.

Brando used his massive bulk to comically menacing effect; and yet at the same time he seemed to be acting in a more serious movie than everybody else and was always on the point of saying something interesting about morality and corruption in Big Business but never quite finding the words: and the words he did find were, more often than not, an incoherent mumble.

The Formula offered such incidental

Marlon Brando in
The Formula

pleasures as two elephants, who lumbered across the screen during the credit titles and were never seen again. There were two crocodiles, who looked as if they hadn't worked since the 1933 *King Kong* and had been brought out of retirement to provide some window dressing. There was also a frog, which surfaced from a chlorine-filled swimming pool to make a brief and incongruous anti-pollution commercial. There was, too, the added bonus of Sir John Gielgud's hilarious German accent, a rare treat for connoisseurs. Gielgud played the inventor of the formula.

George C. Scott, cast as a washed-up-son-of-a-bitch who operated alone, walked through the film as if he were as bored with

176

his role as the audience was. His final confrontation with Brando went for absolutely nothing. It was reported in the press that the director and the author had both tried, unsuccessfully, to get their names removed from the film.

I consider Brando the greatest living American actor on the screen today. His great talent is totally original. He revolutionized film acting and now he has gone even beyond that. Today he has become an impressionist. True, he is not easy for other actors to work with because of his unique performing style, but every actor who has ever shared a scene with Marlon will admit it was a memorable experience.

George C. Scott,
quoted by MGM publicity department

Every time we went through a rehearsal of a long and involved dolly shot, Marlon would improvise new lines as they occurred to him. Finally, with a grin on his face, George said to Marlon: 'Are you ever going to say the same line twice?' Brando just slapped him on the back and replied: 'Doesn't make any difference, George, because I know you know a cue when you hear one.'

John G. Avildsen,
quoted by MGM publicity department

And Marlon Brando (reputedly at $250,000 a day) is worth every penny for his off-the-wall interpretation of the OPEC cartel-in-chief, Steiffel. He makes the role swell with a benign malignancy, a genial giant to whom total ruthlessness is an accepted fact of life. Brando has only three scenes in the movie, but it soars whenever he is present.

Arthur Knight, *The Hollywood Reporter*

George C. Scott and
Marlon Brando in
The Formula

A DRY WHITE SEASON

Directed by Euzhan Palcy   1989

Justice and law can be described as distant cousins and here in South Africa they are not on speaking terms.

Ian McKenzie

A Dry White Season was a well-meaning, earnest campaign film; but like so many propaganda films about South Africa, it fell into the standard clichés of the anti-apartheid movie in which the blacks were nearly all good and the whites nearly all sadistic racists.

The story had its roots in the massacre of the schoolchildren by the police during the 1976 Soweto Uprising and concerned the political conversion of a naive white Afrikaner schoolteacher (Donald Sutherland) whose complacency and passivity were given a jolt when he learned of the torture and death of his black gardener (Winston Tshona) and the torture of the gardener's son and wife, who died while they were in police custody. In seeking to expose the security forces' brutality, the teacher was ostracized by his wife, daughter, headmaster and colleagues.

The scenes of brutality were genuinely shocking; though Jurgen Prochna, in his role of Special Branch Officer justifying murder as being good for the country, seemed to be playing a Nazi villain in one of those old-fashioned World War II melodramas.

Brando (who, it was reported, contributed all his fees to an anti-apartheid organization) felt *A Dry White Season* could have been more effective politically and went on television to complain that, by leaving most of his part on the cutting-room floor, MGM had spoiled the film.

Marlon Brando and Donald Sutherland in *A Dry White Season*

Marlon Brando in
A Dry White Season

His role was Ian McKenzie, a jaded and world-weary human rights lawyer, who took on the case because he wanted to make it abundantly clear that justice in South Africa was misapplied when it came to a question of race. The performance began with some extraneous humour: offers of lozenges ('totally ineffective, but they're rather tasty') and remarks about his allergy to plants. However, once he was in the courtroom, he dominated the action by his authority, acid sarcasm and bulky presence. His ironic cross-examination of a doctor (Paul Brooke) was particularly enjoyable. The acting, expansive and operatic, belonged to a long cinematic tradition of highly theatrical lawyers, which embraces such famous performers as Orson Welles in *Compulsion*, Spencer Tracy in *Inherit the Wind* and Charles Laughton in *Witness for the Prosecution*.

He sometimes seems not so much in a class of his own as in a world of his own.

Hugo Davenport, *Daily Telegraph*

As for Brando, drawling languidly in a bedraggled suit and half-moon spectacles, it is just as well his role was curtailed; a little eccentric barnstorming goes a long way.

Geoff Brown, *The Times*

His greatness as an actor is – as ever – that he breaks all the rules. He mumbles in his chin, he gazes at the ceiling; he peers over jumbo-sized jowls; he plants pauses where they don't belong (as a bomber plants gelignite in a crack in the wall); and he slurs, sneers or detonates with sudden oracular wit. It is as if the mantle of Orson Welles had newly fallen on him from Heaven.

Nigel Andrews, *Financial Times*

180

THE FRESHMAN

Directed by Andrew Bergman   1990

Once you have Marlon in a picture, you're in casting heaven because every actor in the world wants to work with him.

Andrew Bergman

The Freshman was a very enjoyable pastiche Mob movie with a sting in its lizard's tale. Within minutes of his arrival in New York, a young and innocent film student (Matthew Broderick) was robbed of all that he had and found himself working for the Mafia. His boss (Marlon Brando) was an extremely powerful importer, who catered for an international clientele and made millions out of a Gourmet Club at which the only dishes on the menu were endangered species. The freshman's first job was to collect and deliver a Komodo dragon (an Indonesian giant lizard) to the Club's kitchens.

The running gag was that the boss (nickname: Jimmy the Toucan) looked so remarkably like Don Corleone in *The Godfather* that everybody presumed he must have served as the real-life model for the Francis Ford Coppola film, rather than the other way round.

Brando, a massive, Buddha-like statue, rasping to the point of inaudibility and cracking walnuts in a manner which would make any hood fear for his nuts, gave a nicely judged parody of himself, playing the heavy man with the lightest of touches. The student's initial briefing, during which a hood (the admirable Bruno Kirby) kept translating simple Italian phrases anybody could have understood, was very funny.

The best thing about Andrew Bergman's witty script (which made in passing a number of jokes about cineastes) was the relationship between the mobster and the college kid, the son he had never had. The subtle and humorous interplay between the two actors was a pleasure to watch. Broderick, against all the odds, was not annihilated. The affection the older man felt for the youngster was also reciprocated by the audience's own affection for the star.

The satire on Mafia paternalism and mushy sentimentality was deft. There was a kiss on the lips to end all kisses on the lips. The scene, too, where the old man wandered through the market on a royal walkabout, distributing largesse, was a gentle guying of the whole genre, yet so gentle that it might have been missed.

Marlon Brando and Maximilian Schell in *The Freshman*

181

Marlon Brando,
Bruno Kirby,
Penelope Ann Miller
Matthew Broderick
in *The Freshman*

Marlon Brando and
Matthew Broderick
in *The Freshman*

There was a lyrical interlude when Brando went ice-skating. He might not have been Fred Astaire, as the publicity people would have had the public believe, but the scene had magic nevertheless and when the student, who was watching, commented, 'That's nice,' it would have been hard not to agree.

The other star was the Komodo dragon, played by seven lizards, with seven different personalities, who made up one composite dragon. The dragon had a sequence, straight out of a screwball comedy of the 1930s, which began promisingly enough when he was picked up at a warehouse and strapped into a car with a seat belt. The panic, however, which ensued when he escaped, was tame, a disappointing send-up of monster-movie hysteria without the farcical detail to back it up.

Of course, it is Brando who grabs centre screen, balancing the considerable self-parody of his performance with sensitivity, intelligence and even melancholy.

Anne Totterdell, *Financial Times*

Whenever Brando's whale-like presence fills the screen, the film grinds to a halt and smacks not of freshness but of stale, starry self-satisfaction.

Christopher Tookey, *Sunday Telegraph*

To see Brando enjoying himself, but not drowning the joke with any outsize jinks, is a rarity these days. I imagine *The Freshman* will be obligatory viewing for his admirers in years to come – not as a requiem for a screen heavyweight, but as a demonstration of what made Brando a contender in the first place.

Alexander Walker, *Evening Standard*

CHRISTOPHER COLUMBUS – THE DISCOVERY

Directed by John Glen   1992

There were no fewer than three films to celebrate Christopher Columbus's discovery of America in 1498. *Christopher Columbus – The Discovery* arrived first. Then came *Carry on Columbus.* Finally, there was Ridley Scott's *1492: Conquest of Paradise* with Gérard Depardieu. The Ridley Scott, though very disappointing, was easily the best. The other two were dire.

Marlon Brando, cast in the cameo role of Torquemada, the Inquisitor-General, got top billing. Tom Selleck, cast in the fractionally larger part of King Ferdinand of Spain, got second billing. George Corraface, playing the lead, got third billing, his name appearing under the title. Corraface (who would have played the title role in the proposed David Lean version of Joseph Conrad's *Nostromo* had Lean not died before it could be made) spent much of the film with a big grin on his face. It was the sort of grin cinemagoers might have expected to find in an old-fashioned swashbuckling movie, starring either Douglas Fairbanks or Errol Flynn. The characterization was nil. All that could be said about this Columbus was that he wasn't as nice at the end of the film as he had been at the beginning. The nastiness had a tacked-on feeling, as if the producers had realized, somewhat late in the day, that they ran the risk of being politically incorrect.

It might have been thought that between them, Alexander and Ilya Salkind (producers of the *Superman* movies), John Glen (director of the James Bond movies) and Mario Puzo (author of the *Godfather* movies) would have been able to provide a bit more excitement.

But *Christopher Columbus – The Discovery* provided a superficial and banal exercise in epic film-making, moving from cliché to cliché and playing like a parody of the Hollywood history genre. The dialogue was crass. 'You have a way with women, Colon,' said Queen Isabella of Spain (Rachel Ward). 'I'm from Genoa, your highness,' replied the hero. The direction and photography were equally pedestrian. Columbus, clearly anticipating the critical reception of the film, called on God twice to ask Him why He had forsaken him.

The Inquisitor should have been a good role. Tomás de Torquemada (1420-98) was, after all, notorious for the severity of his judgements and the cruelty of his punishments. Brando, in an enormous black robe and black skull cap, played him as a wise old bird, smiling enigmatically while casting gloom and despondency. His office was conveniently situated next door to the torture chamber, through which his victims had to pass to be interviewed by him. Brando had only one scene with any dramatic potential and this was when the Inquisitor questioned Columbus to see if he was a heretic. Unfortunately, nothing came of it. There was never any sense of danger in their confrontation. All Columbus had to do was to quote a bit of science, logic and the Bible and Torquemada gave up. As for his other scenes, there was little for Brando to do except stand around.

Marlon Brando as Torquemada phones his performance in from the Mogadon factory.

Anne Billson, *Sunday Telegraph*

George Corraface, Marlon Brando and Rachel Ward in *Christopher Columbus – The Discovery*

Awards

1951

The American Academy of Motion Picture
Arts and Sciences
   Oscar nomination for Best Actor:
   A Streetcar Named Desire

1952

The American Academy of Motion Picture
Arts and Sciences
   Oscar nomination for Best Actor:
   Viva Zapata!
British Academy
   Best Foreign Actor: *Viva Zapata!*
Cannes Film Festival
   Best Actor: *Viva Zapata!*

1953

The American Academy of Motion Pictures
Arts and Sciences
   Oscar nomination for Best Actor:
   Julius Caesar
British Academy
   Best Foreign Actor: *Julius Caesar*

1954

The American Academy of Motion Picture
Arts and Sciences
   Oscar for Best Actor: *On the Waterfront*
New York Film Critics
   Best Actor: *On the Waterfront*
Hollywood Foreign Press Association
   Golden Globe Best Actor: *On the
   Waterfront*
British Academy
   Best Foreign Actor: *On the Waterfront*

1957

The American Academy of Motion Picture
Arts and Sciences
   Oscar nomination for Best Actor: *Sayonara*

1961

San Sebastian Film Festival
   Golden Conch for Best Feature Film:
   One-Eyed Jacks

1972

The American Academy of Motion Picture
Arts and Sciences
   Oscar for Best Actor (declined):
   The Godfather
Foreign Press Association
   Best Actor: *The Godfather*

1973

The American Academy of Motion Picture
Arts and Sciences
   Oscar nomination for Best Actor:
   Last Tango in Paris
New York Film Critics
   Best Actor: *Last Tango in Paris*

1979

The American Academy of Television Arts
and Sciences
   Emmy for Outstanding Supporting Actor in
   a limited series or a special continuing or
   single appearance: *Roots: The Next
   Generations*

1989

The American Academy of Motion Picture
Arts and Sciences
   Oscar nomination for Best Supporting
   Actor: *A Dry White Season*

Marlon Brando in
The Godfather

Chronology

FILM

DATE	TITLE	ROLE	SCREENPLAY	DIRECTOR
1950	The Men (Alternative title: *Battle Stripe*)	Ken Wilozek	Carl Foreman	Fred Zinnemann
1951	A Streetcar Named Desire	Stanley Kowalski	Tennessee Williams, adapted from his play by Oscar Saul	Elia Kazan
1952	Viva Zapata!	Zapata	John Steinbeck, based on the novel *Zapata the Unconquerable* by Edgcumb Pinchon	Elia Kazan
1953	Julius Caesar	Mark Antony	Joseph L. Mankiewicz, based on play by William Shakespeare	Joseph L. Mankiewicz
1954	The Wild One	Johnny	John Paxton, based on story by Frank Rooney	Laslo Benedek
1954	On the Waterfront	Terry Malone	Budd Schulberg, based on story by Budd Schulberg and articles by Malcolm Johnson	Elia Kazan
1954	Desirée	Napoleon	Daniel Taradash, from the novel by Annemarie Selinko	Henry Koster
1955	Guys and Dolls	Sky Masterson	Joseph L. Mankiewicz, music and lyrics by Frank Loesser, based on Broadway musical, book by Jo Swerling and Abe Burrows, from a Damon Runyon story	Joseph L. Mankiewicz
1956	The Teahouse of the August Moon	Sakini	John Patrick, based on his play and the book by Vern J. Sneider	Daniel Mann
1957	Sayonara	Major Lloyd Gruver	Paul Osborn, based on novel by James A. Michener	Joshua Logan
1958	The Young Lions	Christian Diestl	Edward Anhalt, based on the novel by Irwin Shaw	Edward Dmytryk
1960	The Fugitive Kind	Val Xavier	Tennessee Williams and Meade Roberts, based on the play *Orpheus Descending* by Tennessee Williams	Sidney Lumet
1961	One-Eyed Jacks	Rio	Guy Trosper and Calder Willingham, based on the novel *The Authentic Death of Hendry Jones* by Charles Neider	Marlon Brando
1962	Mutiny on the Bounty	Fletcher Christian	Charles Lederer, based on the novel by Charles Nordhoff and James Norman Hall	Lewis Milestone
1963	The Ugly American	Harrison Carter MacWhite	Stewart Stern, from the novel by William J. Lederer and Eugene Burdick	George Englund
1964	Bedtime Story	Fred Benson	Stanley Shapiro and Paul Henning	Ralph Levy
1965	The Saboteur: Code Name 'Morituri'	Robert Crain	Daniel Taradash, based on the novel *Morituri* by Werner Joerg Luedecke	Bernhard Wicki

1966	The Appaloosa (Alternative title: *Southwest to Sonora*)	Matt	James Bridges and Roland Kibbee, based on the novel by Robert MacLeod	Arthur Penn
1966	The Appaloosa (Alt. title: *Southwest to Sonora*)	Matt	James Bridges and Roland Kibbee, based on the novel by Robert MacLeod	Sidney J. Furie
1967	A Countess from Hong Kong	Ogden	Charles Chaplin	Charles Chaplin
1967	Reflections in a Golden Eye	Major Weldon Penderton	Gladys Hill and Chapman Mortimer, based on the novel by Carson McCullers	John Huston
1968	Candy	Grindl	Buck Henry, based on the novel by Terry Southern and Mason Hoffenberg	Christian Marquand
1969	The Night of the Following Day	Bud	Hubert Cornfield and Robert Phippeny, based on novel *The Snatchers* by Lionel White	Hubert Cornfield
1970	Queimada! (English title: *Burn!*)	Sir William Walker	Franco Solinas and Giorgio Arlorio	Gillo Pontecorvo
1971	The Nightcomers	Peter Quint	Michael Hastings, based on characters from *The Turn of the Screw* by Henry James	Michael Winner
1972	The Godfather	Don Vito Corleone	Mario Puzo and Francis Ford Coppola, based on the novel by Mario Puzo	Francis Ford Coppola
1972	L'Ultimo Tango A Parigi (English title: *Last Tango in Paris*)	Paul	Bernardo Bertolucci and Franco Arcalli	Bernardo Bertolucci
1976	The Missouri Breaks	Robert Lee Clayton	Thomas McGuane	Arthur Penn
1978	Superman	El-Jor	Mario Puzo, David Newman, Robert Benton and Leslie Newman	Richard Donner
1979	Apocalypse Now	Colonel Walter E. Kurtz	John Milius and Francis Ford Coppola, based on the novel *The Heart of Darkness* by Joseph Conrad	Francis Ford Coppola
1980	The Formula	Adam Steiffel	Steve Shagan from his novel	John G. Avildsen
1989	A Dry White Season	Ian McKenzie	Colin Welland and Euzhan Palcy, based on the novel by Andre Brink	Euzhan Palcy
1990	The Freshman	Carmine Sabatini	Andrew Bergman	Andrew Bergman
1992	Christopher Columbus – The Discovery	Torquemada	John Briley and Cary Bates and Mario Puzo	John Glen

THEATRE

DATE	TITLE	ROLE	AUTHOR	DIRECTOR	THEATRE
1943	*Marlon Brando attends Erwin Piscator's Drama Workshop. Productions include:*				
1944	Hannele's Way to Heaven	Gottwald A Great Dark Angel	Gerhardt Hauptmann	Erwin Piscator	
1944	Doctor Sganarelle		Molière	Erwin Piscator	
1944	Twelfth Night	Sebastian	William Shakespeare	Maria Piscator	
1944	Bobino	Giraffe	Stanley Kaufmann	Erwin Piscator	
1944	*Brando's work in the professional theatre begins. All theatres are in New York unless otherwise stated.*				
1944	I Remember Mama	Nels	John Van Druten, from Kathryn Forbes' *Mama's Bank Account*	John Van Druten	Music Box
1946	Truckline Café	Sage McRae	Maxwell Anderson	Harold Clurman	Belasco
1946	Candida	Eugene Marchbanks	Bernard Shaw	Guthrie McClintic	Cort
1946	Antigone	Messenger	Jean Anouilh, translated by Lewis Galantière	Guthrie McClintic	Cort
1946	A Flag is Born	David	Ben Hecht, music by Kurt Weill	Luther Adler	Alvin
1947	The Eagle Has Two Heads	Stanislas	Jean Cocteau, adapted by Ronald Duncan	John C. Wilson	Tour: Washington and Boston
1947	A Streetcar Named Desire	Stanley Kowalski	Tennessee Williams	Elia Kazan	Barrymore
1953	Arms and the Man	Sergius Saranoff	Bernard Shaw	Herbert Ratner	Summer stock: Cooamessett and Ivoryton

TELEVISION

DATE	TITLE	ROLE	AUTHOR	DIRECTOR	COMPANY
1949	I'm No Hero				CBS
1950	Come Out Fighting				NBC
1979	Roots: The Next Generations	George Lincoln Rockwell	Ernest Konoy Sidney A. Glass Thad Mumford Daniel Wilcox John McGreevey	John Erman Charles S. Dubin George Stanford Brown Lloyd Richards	ABC

Acknowledgements

The author would like to begin by thanking Barry Holmes, his editor.

The author and publishers express their appreciation to the Kobal Collection and the following companies for their assistance and/or permission in relation to the following photographs:
The Kobal Collection: frontispiece, pp. 9, 12, 15, 18, 28, 31, 32, 33, 34–5, 36, 37, 40, 44, 45, 46, 48–9, 52–3, 54, 56, 57, 58, 59, 60–1, 62–3, 64, 65, 66–7, 68, 69, 70, 72, 74, 76, 77, 78–9, 80–1, 82, 83, 84, 87, 88, 90, 91, 93, 95, 97, 98–9, 100, 101, 102, 103, 104, 105, 106, 108, 109, 110, 112, 113, 114–15, 116, 118, 120, 122–3, 125, 126, 127, 128, 129, 132, 137, 140–1, 143, 144–5, 146–7, 147, 148–9, 152–3, 155, 156, 157, 158–9, 162, 164, 166, 167, 168–9, 173, 174, 176, 177, 181, 182, 183, 185, 186; BFI Stills, Posters and Designs, pp. 6, 41, 73, 117, 119, 121, 124, 170–1, 178–9, 180, New York Public Library at Lincoln Center: pp. 20, 21, 22; Eileen Darby: pp. 24–5, 27; ABC: p. 173; AVCO Embassy: pp. 132, 140–1, 143; Columbia Pictures: frontispiece, pp. 12, 28, 52–3, 54, 56, 57, 58, 59, 60–1, 110, 111, 112, 113; Metro-Goldwyn-Meyer: pp. 45, 46, 48–9, 71, 72, 95, 97, 98–9, 174, 176, 177; MGM/Samuel Goldwyn: pp. 66–7, 68, 69, 70; Paramount Pictures: pp. 15, 84, 90, 91, 93, 94, 144–5, 146–7, 147, 148–9, 151, 186; Peel Enterprises: p. 185; Selmar Pictures, Dear Films, Corona Films: pp. 126, 127; Tri-Star: pp. 181, 182, 183; Twentieth Century Fox: pp. 42–3, 44, 62–3, 64, 65, 78–9, 80–1, 82, 83, 106, 108, 109; United Artists; pp. 31, 32, 33, 87, 88, 89, 134–5, 136, 137, 138–9, 152–3, 155, 156, 157, 158–9, 160–1, 162, 163; Universal Pictures: pp. 100, 101, 102, 103, 104, 105, 114–15, 116, 118, 119, 120, 121, 128, 129, 130; Warner Bros: pp. 9, 34–5, 36, 37, 40, 74, 76, 77, 164, 165; Warner Seven Arts: pp. 122–3, 124, 125; Zoetrope/United Artists: pp. 166, 167, 168–9, 170–1.

The author would like to add a personal note of thanks to Christine Lloyd Lyons and her staff at the Kobal Collection, to the staff at the Performing Arts Research Center at the New York Public Library and to everybody at the BFT reference library and stills department.

Index